W9-BWA-727

Make Yourself an Ark

Make Yourself an Ark

Beyond the Memorized Responses of Our Corporate Adolescence

Barbara Doherty, S.P.

THE THOMAS MORE PRESS
Chicago, Illinois

ISBN 0-88347-162-0

CONTENTS:

This book is dedicated to my beloved siblings, Patsy and Mary. It is also given to the beautiful people they brought to our family: Ed and Jim; Martin, Sheila, Eddie, Anne, Joe, Meg, and Jamie. It has been joy to journey together.

Gratitude goes to so many from whose support, research, conversations, and arguments came the Ark: Nancy Nolan, Ellen Cunningham, Clarice Asbury, Rosemary Nudd, Sally Thomas, Agnes Mahoney, Ann Sullivan, Jean Alice McGoff, Charles Fisher, and all the audiences who listened to me as the ideas in this book were clarified and confirmed.

Ann Kevin O'Connor and Elizabeth Clare Vrabely untiringly offered their editing and typing skills.

Introduction

"Make yourself an ark of gopherwood, put various compartments in it, and cover it inside and out.... This is how you shall build it.... Make an opening for daylight in the ark... Put an entrance in the side of the ark.... I am about to bring the flood waters on the earth.... But with you I will establish my covenant...."

God to Noah, *Genesis* 6

A grade-school essay entitled, "The Doherty Dogs," chronicled the adventures of five unfortunate canines—Senator, Inky, Wags, Mickey, and Muggins—who found themselves members of the Doherty household for brief periods of time. Except for my father and one sister, the rest of our family were not animal lovers. We wouldn't hurt an animal, but we had some amorphous sense that, as far as we were concerned, the dogs should have stayed in their own world and we in ours.

Because of this separatist mentality toward animals, writing about the journey to the self and into God by means of a Noah's Ark could be a simplistic conceit, cluttering rather than enlightening the journey. Animal metaphors, however, apparently attracted the mystics of our tradition and afforded them certain insights. Since there is a sufficient zoology to enhance our ideas, we bid welcome to that creation which is kin to part of us and invite its untutored, instinctual presence.

I hasten to add that the mystics were not primarily engaged in writing animal stories, but some creatures were evidently useful as characters or participants in the extension of a thought. These animals offer a camaraderie as we study the ways Providence brings us to know the self and to learn that the journey to the self is the same as the journey into God.

I am not a psychologist; thus, I intend to avoid statements about self-knowledge that belong to this discipline. I am attracted to the topic of self-knowledge because of faith seeking understanding, a proper starting place for the person whose work is theology. A scholar-friend, Rosemary Nudd, has suggested that "to know" means to give oneself over to mystery. I shall borrow this as the working definition of "to know the self." When I give myself over to the mysteries hidden deep within and accept what I find there, I have begun the journey to the self which culminates in the revelation the writer of Ephesians knew: I am filled with all the fullness of God.

The title comes from the great flood story in the Book of Genesis. God's bidding can be heard to contain two messages: obviously, the directions given Noah, but beyond that significance, the one the reader has already grasped—the ark is the self with whom God makes covenant. Making the self an ark occurs as we know progressively who we are, through the sometimes gentle, sometimes violent processes that life involves. The resultant personal authenticity is a wonderful and marvelous happening. Without self-knowledge, we wander for years slightly or greatly out of touch with the exquisite uniqueness that is our own truth, goodness, and beauty.

It is, of course, what we hate in ourselves that prevents self-knowledge.. To begin to love what we hate is the pathway to the self; then we can start the task of loving the other who is neighbor or friend. Ultimately we are led to recognize the God who is the Truth of our truth. Paul Scott's sentence in *The Jewel in the Crown* (Volume I of The Raj Quartet), speaks of the evidence of the self-journey in one of his characters: "In herself she was all the explanation I felt she needed. And that is rare, isn't it? To be explained by yourself, by what you are and what you do, and not by what you've done, or were, or by what people think you might be or might become."

Each chapter of this book looks at self-knowledge from a different theological vantage point. The book can be read consecutively, yet the sections also stand as single essays. It reflects the thesis that as a People we are being brought by a wonderful Providence beyond the memorized responses of our corporate adolescence. Aided by the messages of our animal friends, we look at the ark which we are and with whom God is making covenant once again in human history.

CHAPTER ONE

Leviathans and Minnows

God: "Once you but lay a hand upon Leviathan,
no need to recall any other conflict!"

Job: "I have dealt with great things that I do not
understand; things too wonderful for me,
which I cannot know."

40/31; 42/3.

JOB had everything to learn; he presumed he had all the right answers he would need to guide himself and his family through the shoals and reefs of their history. But he hadn't understood about Leviathan, and only after he came up against monstrous conflicts was Job able to reorient his daily journeys and undertake the one and only journey of any importance: the journey to the self which is at once the journey into God.

To know the self. It sounds so simple. The wise have taught that knowing the self is the path to human wholeness and holiness. Surely ignorance of the self cannot constitute such a barrier to maturity that without self-knowledge, one is prevented from the journey to integrity? The answer seems to be yes. Self-knowledge is a desired objective, yet it remains too often merely an espoused value. The cost is great because self-chosen hypocrisies afford pleasant, familiar safety zones. We are comfortable with platitudes, pseudo-directions, and old worn-out behavior patterns. Something plagues us, however; we have an unformulated sense that knowing who we are is important for those of us who have to shovel snow, who get chest pains from tension, who wait for buses, and who refuse to buy from firms that have unfair hiring practices. We may not name that which we're searching for "self-knowledge," but we know that without personal integrity, the resources with which we face life are meager and paltry.

The mythical sea-monster Leviathan is used by writers of the Wisdom literature to personify the watery and primeval chaos into which the Creator breathed form and meaning. One is given to understand early on that Yahweh has power over the monster of the deep; God can feed this creature to the sharks! We know formlessness and chaos to be part of who we are, yet when we are sailing calm seas we have some halcyon feeling that all is under control. It is only when we spy the shadow of Leviathan lurking just beneath the surface water that we are overwhelmed by the inevitability of yet another conflict with some monster we neither desire to encounter nor wish to understand.

Leviathan signifies all the conflicts which oddly enough are the only means by which we can break through petty illusions and cast-iron antipathies into a self-possession which enlightens the prosaic with new dimensions. Ancient sailors didn't like meeting gargantuan whales any better than we like coming up against oppositions inside and outside ourselves, yet it is precisely these obstacles to our ordinary ways of doing and thinking things that bring us to know the self. Without Leviathan we really never change. For reasons hidden deep within the human condition, the antecedent to the self-journey is this confrontation. The monsters force us to examine our paths, our statements, our thoughts, and our processes. But why? Why can't we get from Point A to

Point B in our maturation process without conflict? I asked this question of a psychologist and colleague, Ann Sullivan, only to receive the answer: "Original sin." I wanted psychological illumination and was ushered back to the answers of my own discipline. Somehow lurking deep in the creation is the mystery of personal and corporate disorientation and ignorance and the need for salvation. Creation and salvation form the two-yet-utterly-one divine action that is redemptive. The chaotic in me and in us as a people is saved by the very act of creation. This creation is not a one-time happening that God set in motion; it is a continuing divine intervention to save, right within the details of our daily history as it is created.

Wisdom teachers have tried to point out the ordinariness of the journey to the self and into God, but we have a propensity to aggrandize devotional happenings and to long for anything weird or peculiar to label religious. We can then relegate devotion to those who are weird or peculiar. Leviathan is the ordinary absurdity in us as it comes up against the ordinary and extraordinary absurdity around us. The conflict can compel us to the great lessons of wisdom: If we bend, we will not break. If we are emptied, we can be filled. Jesus emptied himself, became obedient to the irrationalities of providence including a scandalous death and gave humankind a way to interpret the irrationalities of each day and to invest them with redemptive significance.

Our first instinct is to reject this thinking as nothing other than calling "religious" what is just part of life. Everybody has ups and downs. To bend, to be emptied, to be obedient to the circumstances of the day—such phrases are nothing other than mealy-mouthed acceptance of pain. We will not be doormats. We do not have to make life any harder than it is by looking for hardship. That's absolutely true. The circumstances which wind circuitously through our days constitute all the absurdity we will ever need for our human maturation. From the first contradiction of the day: "We'll leave at 3." "No, at 2," we're off and running through the confrontations with minnows and sea-monsters. Some are inconsequential happenings and are merely the give and take of the day though not less annoying. But some monsters swim too close to our boats: "Don't do it that way." "You're wrong." These behemoths challenge our self-image to its foundation and impute to us the most stupid and awkward ways of proceeding. They tell us that everything we have believed about the self is erroneous.

The enigma is that the challenges are both correct and inaccurate. We are often utterly on the right track, yet there is that about us which is chaotic and unformed. Behavior is out of line and proceeds from disordered directions deep within.We are sometimes vaguely aware of our disorientation, but most often only conflict causes it to surface. Leviathan has many forms: physical and mental illnesses in us and in loved ones, aging, relationships broken by death or misunderstandings, global violence. The work involved in ascertaining the significance of Leviathan impels us along the journey to self-knowledge.

It is a precarious journey. We lie to ourselves about who we are and about our motivations with the greatest candor and conviction. Sometimes our defenses against pain are so fragile that we retreat from the self and hide from the threats against who we have named ourselves to be. For some of us, the self-image is so poor and we are so self-defeated that we have needed to distort reality to preserve some shred of sanity. Only the truth of self-knowledge can make us free. When we begin the journey, we can admit the distortions in ourselves, yet know in faith that we are saved and touched by grace with the utmost love. Then only do we find new growth possibilities and deeper purposes.

The biggest barrier to self-discovery is the vast store-house of manipulative techniques that we display as soon as we sniff the scent of the fish in the water:

"I'm wasting your time."

"You've never been on my side anyway."

"You've never understood me."

"You hate me."

"There is nothing I can do."

We drown in the foolishness of these negative assertions. We garner our lies, assert their truth, and pretend to start new paths which bear the traces of our previous foot-prints. The pain of watching persons deny the journey to the truth of the self is frightening. The choice for stagna-tion through self-deception seems an impossible human option, yet the evidence is staggering within and outside ourselves. The manipulator in us capably sloughs off any personal responsibility for confronting Leviathan. For a time at least the monster swims off leaving us with what-ever puny resources we had before the potential conflict. We have refused challenge and change because the battle looked too great. "Perhaps if I discovered the self, there would be nothing there. If I changed from my usual ways of doing things, I would not be who I am." The most pathetic manipulators of reality use religious language to approve their deceptions: It is God who has shown how to circumnavigate Leviathan!

We are not pathological cases but ordinary people who live in houses, apartments, condos, and rectories. We protect ourselves from the conflicts that lead to self-knowledge. The phrase "journey to knowing the self" makes us dig up our old fears and self-hatred. What we have learned about ourselves frightens us and makes us abandon the journey to the center. Perhaps somewhere long ago, we received a message that we were worthless, and we have never been able to move very far beyond the destructiveness of that disapprobation. We have clung to it as the foundation of who we are: "the rejected one." Hamlet's insight, "Fie on't! ah fie! 'Tis an unweeded garden that grows to seed," warns that our discontents, self-hatred, rages, and fears can become what constitutes the entire garden.

Karl Rahner speaks of humanity as an indefinability coming to consciousness of itself. We accept or reject what is indefinable about us. When we choose rejection, we move farther away from self-knowledge; when we accept who and what we are, the journey to interiority is underway.

Sometimes church rules, as we have learned and interpreted them, reinforce self-hatred. We are married "outside the church" and thus outside the pale of moral acceptability. We plan our families. The doom of eternal sanction, let alone being at odds with the rules, tells us what we already knew anyway: We are no good. The question of our sexual identity haunts us. Could we possibly be what our society despises? Something we did long ago causes us to recoil from the pain we brought to another. When we have looked into ourselves and seen what is there, we choke on our own self-hatred.

Note that many "evils" we perceive in ourselves pertain to us as sexual beings. This fact should give us some clue about our disorientations and should lead us to question what our hidden guilts and anxieties have to do with the following of Jesus. We prefer, however, to waste years blaming our grade-school teachers and the "system" for what it taught or did not teach about life. While we are bemoaning our sexual peccadillos, our omission of Sunday worship, the changes in the church, or the last time we went to confession, we have no concept of such a thing as a journey to the self or to that authenticity and maturation we must achieve as human beings if we are ever to know God. There is nothing, absolutely nothing about us, that God's love does not use redemptively. It is we who cling to our misshapen evasions because these are like a pair of broken-in thongs that don't hurt our toes; the new pair will take some getting used to. It might be a totally different world if we let go of the infantile religious notions we've clung to as the substance of who we are. Our seventh-grade teacher has perhaps matured into a wise and holy human being while we are still back in seventh grade emotionally and spiritually.

The "sin against the Holy Spirit," or the "unforgivable sin" has been defined as our electing to call light, darkness. This translates in simple terms that light comes and we see avenues out of our present ruts. We know some truths about who we are and where we're going, but we deliberately choose to say, no, there is no light. We plant weeds in the garden and call them flowers. We resist self-knowledge over and over again. We reject the mystery of the indefinabilities that lie at the center of the self. We are terrified of the truth. We prefer lies enhanced by the guilt derived from the moral exhortations of church persons. The sin is "unforgivable" because we have made it so. We have chosen deceit as reality.

There is a slang expression: "to be full of baloney."
When we acknowledge the quantity of this luncheon meat
in the self, we are on the way to self-knowledge. The
biggest excuse for postponing the journey is to blame our
present, static position on others. "They" did this to me.
Erica Jong has told us our dread of self-responsibility. I
alone am responsible for my life. The personal discovery
of the paradigm of following Jesus today within the community of believers lies ahead for my choice and commitment.

We say to runners: "Go for it!" We must say to ourselves regarding the journey to self and into God—"Go
for it!" Leave off the banal exonerations that impede.
Just as we are, just who we are, limitations and foolishnesses, gifts and talents, we undertake the journey. We
need help from counselors, directors, and friends, but we
can't let ourselves be deceived by specious desires to keep
repeating threadbare vindications to new listeners. A
prayer for strength, a last fond look at the baloney and
we must be off. Go for it!

If the love of God means anything at all beyond pious
affection, it means that in all our foolishness, God intervenes historically to redeem and save. We so like to
believe that God comes only when we are functioning
splendidly in our own eyes, but God's entry occurs when
someone lets us know we're not all bad and that there is
much that is beautiful and good about us. We can begin
to assert that we are worth something despite failure
and futility.

These ideas do not bless and condone sin. Sin is sin.
Drug dealers who sell narcotics to the poor on the streets
of our slums are sin. The harm we have inflicted on ourselves and others is sin. Usually however, we lie to our-

selves about the real sin in us and rest content with ineffectual guilt from which we derive some odd tingle of
atonement. We wound and cheat and wallow in our guilt.
Only when we see and move through these intricately
camouflaged externals to the self in truth and humility,
can we find reality beneath the mounds of scripts we have
written to ward it off. We reach a self-possession beyond
our efforts at redeeming ourselves and live with the faith
that, in our sin, it is God who saves. God is in charge of
Leviathan after all.

Leviathan causes us to change if, after the battle, we
make the new decisions and assume the new directions
which the grace of conflict offers. We like only easy graces,
of course. We appreciate the kinds that swim like minnows gently and painlessly into our days. Even the dark
shadow of Leviathan in the water makes our heart skip a
beat and tempts us to sail for shore: "Do not put a harpoon
in my hand," we shout to life, "perhaps the beast and I
might talk." But the sea-monster contraverts all our
schemes and forces us to assess our personal resources
for the battle.

What is it that happens through conflict? Why is Leviathan the antecedent to self-knowledge? When we come up
against the small and the great things that cause us pain,
we are forced to choose either life or death. We can forego
any further efforts at life, or we can shift gears into new
ways of dealing with reality. This is not merely a natural
human direction after pain-filled times. It is a journey
undertaken in faith to the core of our being, a journey to
God. We have no comprehension of its meaning. We do
not even name the force that impels, God, until somehow
it strikes us that it is not we who have so successfully
planned the details of the years. Small events encircle

us, and events of global injustices surround us with incredible violence. We can allow a kind of psychological numbness to engulf our personality and live merely fending off what hurts or trying to hide from it. But if, after a particular monster swims off, we shift into a totally different way of perceiving reality and ask what we know about the self from the encounter, then over many years, we can begin to see we've made some progress toward identifying our angers, our hurts and our foolishnesses. More importantly we can allow that these powerful feelings are all right and are the pieces and parts of the indefinable mystery of who we are. If we try to hide who we are from ourselves with some religious vestures or social conventions, then we lag along for years outside the mystery of the self. We do not know; we do not give ourselves over to mystery.

The trappings of religion often prevent the journey to the self when in fact religion ought to be singularly about the journey to the self and into God. But for some venerable reasons, most people seem happy breathing incense, clacking sticks, and mumbling phrases that lull us into feelings of devotion. We hate it when religion demands that our life practices be changed. We parade off to church with our new hats and our polished shoes, treading upon the outstretched hands of the poor along the way. These poor who know their need of salvation stand all around us, but we can't be bothered with the humble and unwashed. "Straighten up and fly right," we say to the indolent who are not in control of their lives. "Get religion!" "Put a nickel in the drum and you'll be saved."

The truth is that the only really religious people around are those who have undertaken the journey to the self. These persons cross all boundaries of lifestyles. They are mothers and nuns, architects and service personnel. There are also mothers and nuns, architects and service personnel who content themselves with vague pieties which avoid finding out too much about the self. God forbid that we should discover Leviathan right in the depths of our own unconscious! Conflict permits us the discovery of the self. Grace enables us to enter the conflict and to come out of it choosing life. In conflict, we see our motivations; if we're honest, conflict occasions the possibilities for the purification and refining process of our humanity.

We all wish there were another way to self-knowledge. There isn't. We can wish and hope and shut our eyes against Leviathan, but it will lurk around us until we face it. Our dark shadows are redeemed and redemptive; they are the stuff of our salvation. The mystics have always known this. We can sing and dance and march all the way to the church building and back, but our journeys to church are substantive only if they express and mirror the journey to the self.

Focus is imperative for the journey to the self. Reality is not here and there and everywhere. It is one. It is our life. It is who we are. Integrity is the key. Conflict forces us to knowledge of the self or forces us away from it. Because of this dual possibility, we must reflect upon the conflicts in our lives, personal, relational, and global. Through serious reflection, we can trace the lines of our personal and communal salvation history. In all our ups and downs, God was present to save even when we had no devotional feelings whatsoever. We were led to life and change, or we chose death and closed the door on maturation. If we did that, we know we have to go back to that door and open it, no matter the cost. Only then is the integrity of the journey to the self assured. Without reflection, conflict becomes meaningless. We spear one whale after another, but they keep on coming. None of them offers any message. We know only weariness, tedium, and despair. Within the community of Jesus' disciples we are able to assess the meaning of conflict and confront it together, seeking always the meaning of the life of Jesus as it unfolds in our lives. "No sign will be given this evil age except the sign of Jonah. Just as Jonah was a sign for the Ninevites, so will the Son of Man be a sign for the present age."

The church gathers together to name Leviathan and thus to overcome its power to destroy. We have been brought by God's doing beyond the memorized responses of our corporate adolescence as a church people. Formerly we might have been content with our cleverness in explicating our doctrines.Foes would stand in awe of our clear-cut and impregnable defense of the faith. No matter that beyond the verbiage might lie no understanding whatsoever of the following of Jesus or of what such discipleship would cost us personally.

By a wonderful mystery of Providence, the journey to the self appears to us now to be the bedrock of our Christian understanding. Without self-knowledge, church-attendance or devotional and sacramental practice lack foundation. Self-knowledge is the basis for wholeness and holiness. The journey to the self allows us the possibility to become Jesus once again in human history and this, right in and not ever outside, the ordinary conflictual situations of each day. We may hope only for minnows and, as is the nature of minnows, there are often more of them than our psychic nets can contain. Nonetheless, their size makes them appear manageable. Not so

Leviathan. This monster of the deep threatens the outline of our present self-image. Yet only in contending with Leviathan and in wresting from conflict its wisdom, do we become persons who pray, who love, who sing songs and dance, who are whole even in our complexities, who laugh and who weep. We are women and men who can look in hindsight at the Leviathans and know that we were dealing with great things we did not understand and with things that were too wonderful for us which in the moment we did not recognize as evidences of a divine care. Job and his family have become our companions.

CHAPTER TWO

Snakes and Vipers

> "And it will be even impossible for them to stay
> where they are without danger, even though they
> have entered the castle, for in the midst of such
> poisonous creatures one cannot help but be bitten
> at one time or another."
>
> Teresa of Avila in *The Interior Castle*

"SNAKES and Vipers" is a dreadful title, but Teresa of
Avila uses the metaphor of these poisonous reptiles to
typify the disordered conditions in the first mansion of
her seven-mansioned journey to interiority. The person
in this first stage is not a bad person but merely one not
yet ready to be bothered with the serious business of
spiritual journeying. The animals signify all the banal
ruses which we allow to impede the journey to the self
and to God. We welcome the snakes and vipers when we
refuse to ask deeper questions or face any of our paralyz-
ing uncertainties. Teresa knew that only by confronting
the snakes and vipers does one begin the journey to the
self and beyond, to God. We like to choose every other
option: We run outside the inner house and let the snakes
and vipers take over. We haggle with our neighbors about
snakes and vipers discussing their sizes and shapes. We
hide in a small corner allowing the snakes and vipers the
free run of the place. We lie to ourselves for years about
the nonexistence of any such pestilence inside of us. One
day we must look squarely at the snakes and vipers, give
them our name, and admit their identity with the shadow
side of ourselves. We begin the journey to God by accept-

24

ing the mystery of our own oddities, sin, and disorientations as well as the mystery of our own purposes, integrity, and grace.

It is our experience that we usually select every futile way of dealing with the reptilic invasion before we will yield to the mystery of its presence. Our fears, shallowness, self-contempt, excuses, rigid controls, manipulations, boredom, and deceits prevent the journey to interiority or to the giving of ourselves over to the mystery of who we are. We dally over beginning the true journey to God because we deceive ourselves about the self. We even concoct intricate ways of dealing with God which circumvent the task of self-knowledge. We say our prayers, sing our songs, and do our charities—all neatly separated from the arduous journey to the self. The task of interiority awaits us, and we neglect it to our own peril as human beings. The wisdom is constant: we will only know God to the degree we have come to know ourselves.

The gospel tells us that we may gain the whole world but that it will profit us nothing if we destroy ourselves in the process. If we read, "suffer the loss of our souls," the final denouement seems far off, and we can postpone dealing with this remote consequence of our deeds. With a different reading we recognize we are talking about the loss in the immediate moment of our self-identity as followers of Jesus. In the futility of gaining everything, which often takes the form of controlling and programing what we will allow to happen in or to us, we forget who we are and we destroy ourselves because our meaning is dependent on what we can control or manipulate outside of ourselves.

The need for interiority will haunt us, however obscurely, until we begin the journey. Certain unmistakable signs tell us that our present directions are skewed; a psychologist may grace our indisposition with the name depression. We feel an indescribable sense of loss as our solidified worldviews crumble. We are afraid of the self or the no-self that is, or perhaps is not, behind our masks. We run from the dread feelings only so long before anxiety overcomes us, and we are forced to ask ourselves what we're doing and why, where we're going and why, and whether the whole enterprise of our existence has any significance. The anonymity of the final grave overtakes us; it seems to be ready for us before we are ready for the choices death demands of us humans. We call upon our former pieties about heaven and hell to give substance to our lives, but we find ourselves neither renewed and strengthened nor scared and frightened enough to change. Some days we feel as though we're drowning in the sea of the vapid illusions to which we've clung.

This occurrence is more than a "mid-life crisis." It is a crisis of religious meaning and experience. It signals that the spiritual journey is at the point where it is to move steadfastly within, or at the point where a decision is made to chuck the entire enterprise in a futile gesture of despair. The crisis leads to fidelity and holiness or to failure and the destruction of the self. Pop psychology has informed us that taking the time to know the self or paying the price it costs is an unselfish movement toward integrity and maturation. We are beginning to learn that without the journey to the self, and thus to God, any churchly enterprise with all its projects is a vain motion however pious.

In very simple words—if I've lied to myself all of my life about what I and my religious process are all about, then all of my godly or ecclesial postures are phantoms of my own mind. If my life's journey is not issuing in human maturity, wholeness, and integrity and in an ever-growing concern for the world in which I live, then my most devout forays toward eternity are indeed illusory. Struggling with life and ideas, with relationships and decisions are signs of vitality and religious health; the presence of Leviathan is the best indication of the basic goodness of the religious journey. Life is not a somnolent state of inactivity and repose and neither is religion. The authentic religious journey is grounded in the journey to the truth of who I am.

This statement is not some current fad brought to us by those who view the Second Council of the Vatican as the watershed of human history. Women and men of the contemplative tradition, in and outside Christianity, welcomed self-knowledge often won at the expense of change, upset, and redirection to unfamiliar paths. They chose the path to knowledge of the self because they knew, what we are surmising, that the journey to the self is the same journey as that to God. Local scoffers and religious persons called their insight pretentious if not pathological or heretical. What a celebration one might imagine beyond the grave when all contemplatives will be rejoicing that the personal unity and integrity they sought is, in fact, God's name!

Bonaventure explained that the journey to the self is the same journey as that to God by teaching that the image of God is irrevocably struck upon human creation. Though hidden and tarnished with sin, that image was indelibly placed upon the being of a woman or a man. Holiness lay in the revelation of that image as it was gradually clarified through the decisions and choices of each day. As one discovers the true self, one discovers simultaneously the divine presence. In the *Journey of the*

Soul into God, Bonaventure illustrated the stages of this illumination with the metaphor of the six-winged seraph. In each of the six movements to enlightenment, the woman or man journeys into God through knowledge of the self. "Through these lights exteriorly given (i.e., the vestiges of God in the Universe and in the sense world), we are disposed to re-enter the mirror of our mind in which divine realities shine forth."

For Bonaventure, the place to begin the journey inward was "a burning love of Jesus Christ crucified." Does this rhetoric hold any clues for our own journey to illumination? In Jesus the Christ, the image is the perfection of unity with the Godhead; in us, the profound, inexplicable mystery of our baptism moves us to that unity through adoption as daughters and sons. We learned about being "adopted" from our catechisms; it seemed a nice phrase but somehow second-best. We've had to learn anew to look at this doctrine of adoption of humanity by divinity as precisely what the incarnation and thus what each of us is all about. Our movement toward divinity is not the loss of what is most natural to us but rather the evolving of humanity into its primary significance. As our personal integration occurs through the very prosaic episodes of each day—diapers, two-year-olds, and the dents in the car we've saved for—the unity of human and divine is taking place in us as it is eternally in the One who is uniquely and supremely Son. This means that all our puny journeying and the weariness of it, the lights of our days and the boredom of them, are all somehow caught up in what God is all about. We look to our days as revelatory of the divine precisely in what is utterly, obviously, and always human.

We face absurdities each day, in and around us. These

indefinable confusions and complexities weigh us down with a heaviness which dulls our purposes and visions. However, when God's wisdom causes us to make the connection in our minds that all life's ambiguities and struggles are somehow mysteriously the content of redemption, then we are able to look at what happens to us with different eyes. One day a mysterious transfer occurs in us. We begin to see our ups and downs connected with the death and resurrection of Jesus. Every day we die; and in all the wonderful, resurrecting things that happen to us, every day we are raised up. Thus for us "the burning love of Jesus Christ crucified" is not a comforting, mellow feeling about how much Jesus did for us long ago, but rather the welcoming embrace of the details of Jesus' life as we recognize them in our own passovers from death to life. For us, too, the burning love of Jesus Christ crucified is the beginning of the journey, but only as this religious language translates into connection with the commonplace.

Faith illumines our daily circumstances. The journey to the self and into God is underway because the mundane details of life get into focus with the mystery of Jesus. It is not that I so quickly identify what occurs daily with the redemptive mystery. Not at all! It takes me a long, long time to discover meaning in the ordinary, but when I do I have arrived at the beginning stage of illumination and of human maturation. It may feel odd at first, but gradually the faith assessment of my days reveals them as radically connected to enlightenment and wisdom. I am woman. I am man. By God's grace, I have begun the journey to knowing the self; I am in touch with who I am just as I am on this ordinary Monday or Tuesday.

Excessive investigation of my every psychological

stirring is not the point. Though I must be in touch with my feelings, the earth does not revolve around me nor is the world waiting to know why I'm angry, sad, hurt, or irritated. It's wonderful, of course, if a kind friend or loved one allows me to tell of my emotional ups and downs, but the journey to the self is different from endless emotional introspection and narcissistic preoccupation.

The word which best sums up what the ordinariness of our days is all about is the word, weakness. If we begin to know the self at all, what we find there is the inability to carry off most of the grandiose schemes we can devise about practically anything. This does not mean that I cannot get the washing done on Tuesday, nor does it mean I can't carry off a particularly difficult and requiring business deal, or write an intelligent speech, or organize the grade-school children in the cafeteria, or carry off a political campaign. No, the weakness we are discussing is the scriptural message that speaks of power only in weakness. It is the power and weakness of the Passion of Jesus. It is the power one finds in possessing no power. It is the power of life found in death. It is the power of presence found in abandonment.

The journey to the self is the same as the journey to God because what we must acknowledge ultimately about the self is its powerlessness and weakness. When we know the self, we know we have no power of our own to get rid of the snakes and vipers. All the "Anonymous" groups—alcoholics, gamblers, overeaters, the emotionally bogged down, drug users, etc.—work from this principle, but all of us must acknowledge that we have no power to save ourselves. It is only in a glaringly truthful recognition of this spiritual teaching gained through self-knowledge that we will experience the power of God.

To know the self is a requiring task because we work against all our unconscious deceptions. It takes a long time, with the snakes and vipers omnipresent and persistent. Often our admitting the "power greater than ourselves" is still one of our own manipulations. The truth of the religious experience of God's power operative in human weakness means there is nothing of our own machinations left. No one of us can be glib about the radical nature of that sentence, yet we have had the religious gall to call ourselves weak and God powerful when the sentence in our mouths is yet one more piece of self-deception calculated to get some mileage out of human sympathy.

We have recollections of successfully pulling ourselves up by our bootstraps, but if we examine these moments with hindsight a power greater than our own never left our sides during very trying days. In our better moments we can acknowledge the mysterious presence which we all too facilely call God's love. One day the profound meaning of that love will overwhelm us. God's power has filled what is only weakness and powerlessness. Power and Wisdom, titles given to Jesus are part of who we are, too. This is not because we become powerful and wise by dint of personal efforts, but because we have gained a fundamental awareness that God is the Truth of our authenticity, the Power of our personal victories and the Wisdom of our integrations—just as God is all of these in Jesus. Whatever truth we attain about ourselves is attained because God is Truth. Whatever power we feel over against the demonic in and around us is God's Power. Whatever wisdom comes in moments of integrity occurs within that Wisdom which is God's name, whether we define these moments of human maturation with religious language or not. Only faith assures a woman or man of the rightness of these assertions.

The word in spiritual literature for the acknowledgement of a power greater than ourselves is humility, a virtue which welcomes the radical truth of who we are. *Humus* = the earth. Unfortunately, our connotation of this character-strength has been flawed by images of foolish obsequiousness. Teresa of Avila knew humility and truth as synonymous. We are of the earth. We are biodegradible. Seventy percent of our bodies is water like to the waters of the great seas. We are born; we contract illnesses. We return to the earth of which we are composed. All this process is good and natural. Into our humus God placed intellectual and rational possibility. Life, spirit, and grace are ours by a providential disposition. We are of the earth and of heaven all at once.

When pretense and illusion constitute the cornerstone of the self-image, then the truth of weakness and death is outside our grasp. Scripture tells that the lie distorts reality, but with that peculiar oddity rooted in the human condition, we insist upon the benign possibilities of snakes and vipers. We assert our comfortability to the far right or left of the center of the self. Humility compels us to truth and wars against our evasions because earth-life (*humus*), if we live it truly, forces us out of our mental and emotional cocoons and up against what is. If we get walloped by life often enough it should lead us to the truth of the self, to our own powerlessness and to humility. We really aren't the cat's meow or the bee's knees! When we get to the precipice of humility and truth, however, we frequently choose to return to our old ruses. Better our worn lies than leaping into Unknowing. Bonaventure quoting Dionysius warns us: "But you, my friend, concerning mystical visions, with your journey more firmly determined, leave behind your senses and intellectual activities, sensible and invisible things, all nonbeing and being; and in this state of unknowing be restored, insofar as is possible, to unity with God." The journey to the self is the same as the journey into God.

We sigh at the difficulty of locating a proper religious language. How find words which tell the experience of weakness and of empowerment by the divine without sounding like we have abandoned God-given human responsibility? How avoid language which seems to depict us languishing and whining in our powerlessness while the life of discipleship awaits our seizing life and getting on with it?

The razor-thin distinction between the truth of what humanity is and any pretense at powerlessness is the wisdom we must gain. We err always in grasping the precision of the distinction, but when we touch it we are aware of its veracity. Humility is a correct assessment of our reality. We know who we are. The journey to the self is on target. No whining, no illusion here—truth and humility have met in the center of personal existence. We are redeemed from foolish and false directions. We accept the mystery of creation with the image of God impressed forever upon it as well as the further revelation in Jesus that we are daughter or son. Self-knowledge means that we have given ourselves over to the mystery of powerlessness. We cannot solve life—our own or anyone else's. We cannot make things turn out right, people or situations; time and time again we come up against absurdity, particularly our own, and have yielded to its ponderous nonsense.

Only in the acceptance of our powerlessness, weakness,

or infirmity have we any grasp at all of the mystery of the Christian life. St. Augustine's insight that he would understand divinity when he understood the weakness of Jesus has everything to do with the point here. We will try and try to make ourselves Christians by dint of good deeds. But we will be becoming Christians in the fullest and deepest sense when we move on the journey to the self in knowing and acknowledging our own weakness. There we touch the Power that saves, the Power that is at our center, the Power that, in the journey to the self, is the Ground of the journey.

We must know weakness if we are to know power. Paradoxical language either enlightens or frustrates. The paradox of power in weakness is either enlightening or frustrating to who we presently understand ourselves to be. Competent and controlling types hate to admit any chink in the armor of personal power. But we will be brought to powerlessness, like it or not. It is the only way to salvation. The journey to the truth, to humility, to our own weakness through the very ordinary circumstances of each day is the journey to God. There is no other. All other piety is to be preparation for this or it is illusion. Sunday worship can go on for years—even daily communion— without the Christian ever recognizing that s/he has not even begun the religious journey.

The mystery of powerlessness has nothing to do with successful or unsuccessful job performance. It has nothing to do with lackadaisical and shiftless attitudes about our world and its accumulated hopelessness. The most competent, successful, and involved human being may know most truly the meaning of human weakness. The most incompetent who cry "weakness" may be those who cling to their own futile powers over against letting go into God's providential directions.

The trouble with discussing power and weakness is that it is so easily misconstrued. Anyone who wants an excuse for lollygagging through life can come up with the old "power in weakness" ploy and expect applause for indolence. We are not talking about laziness, shabby ministerial efforts, or a n'er-do-well spirituality. This very basic spiritual insight is almost impossible to describe. It frightens the young and inexperienced since it seems to portend failure and futility. It exonerates the lazy or psychically paralyzed from taking hold of life. It offers too facile an excuse for all of us when we wish to shift responsibility from ourselves. And yet: God's power is made known in human weakness. The journey to the self is to result in this revelation.

The worst fact about powerlessness is that it isn't something we can "do." We can't read about it and then decide to "get powerless." Only living life teaches one the power of God made total and whole in human weakness. There is no way one can mime or mimic humility or weakness. It is the most profound acknowledgement of one's life. All pretense is gone. Any imitations of Uriah Heep, no matter how adequate, have palled over against the truth of the mystery. Jesus is the model. His paradoxes confront:

—"Now the hour has come for the Son of Man to be crucified" (Jn 12:23).

—"I have come that you may have life and have it to the full" (Jn 10:9).

—"God sent the Son into the world that through Him the world might be saved" (Jn 3:17).

—"And when I am lifted up from the earth, I shall draw all to myself" (Jn 12:28).

—"Anyone who loves life loses it" (Jn 12:25).

—"Unless a wheat grain falls on the ground and dies, it remains only a single grain" (Jn 12:24).

—"After three days the Son of Man will rise again" (Mk 34).

—"Jesus stretched out his hand, touched him and said, 'Of course, I want to! Be cured!' " (Lk 5:13).

—"I have glorified you on earth and finished the work that you gave me to do" (Jn 17:4).

—"One can have no greater love than to lay down one's life for one's friends" (Jn 15:13).

—"They jeered at him. 'He saved others let him save himself if he is the Christ of God, the Chosen One' (Lk 23:35).

—"Anyone who does not carry the cross and come after me cannot be my disciple" (Lk 14:27).

In these words is life. Without this gospel as the structuring vision of one's religious life, there is really no spiritual journey at all. The words I have used to describe this mystery need not be the words by which another acknowledges the same mystery. Hopefully, there is enough similarity to communicate the truth that the journey to the self is the same as the journey to God because stamped upon us in our weakness is the image of God. When we experience our *humus*, we are filled with God's power. We are empowered beyond natural zest. Here is the mystery of holiness and the great wisdom of Christianity. The experience of weakness is the epitome of human, and thus divine, maturation and is so far away from anything that smacks of being obsequious that it is impossible to put such banal phrases next to this enlightenment. God's power fulfilled and completed in our weakness has nothing to do with human adequacy or the

lack of it. It has to do with the shattering experience of
knowing the self. It is only in this truth that we can stand
in compassion and solidarity with another human being.
Without this normative insight, we will always be persons
who "do for" but who have never known how to "stand
with." We can donate groceries and money to settlement
houses until our shelves are empty; but it is we who must
be empty, and it is we who must be the donation.

A final caution: This wisdom can allow the faulty interpretation welcomed by oppressors who keep people
powerless, while they, the mighty of this world, scorn such
futile humility. One can only ask that this formative
wisdom be grasped in its truth. It does not keep people
down nor is it an opium for people against which right-
minded women and men concerned for justice must
unite. Nothing of the power-in-weakness understanding
halts the work of social justice. Without it, however,
activists among us will find ourselves gradually turning
to despair since so many of the social constructs for which
we struggle are thwarted by the sin and evil present in us
and in society. When this revelation becomes the basis of
who we understand ourselves to be, however, then our
energies for justice remain unflagging against all kinds of
impossible obstacles whether churchly or societal. Only
mystics continue the work of justice without cease because they view reality from a totally different perspective.
Furthermore, they don't sit back and whine when injustice prevails, but are always in the front lines of social
reform. The power that keeps them there is not an energy
of which those with thyroid deficiencies are deprived but
rather the power that is God's presence impelling. In
everyday terms we can perceive this power-in-weakness

when we are ready to quit, to despair, or to become cynical forever, but a power greater than ourselves forces us to continue. Now no longer our own adequate schemes and ideas, but our puny and competent efforts graced beyond imagining. We have been dragged by the hair of our heads to the spiritual journey beyond our own calculations.

This explanation of reality is of absolute necessity to the journey to the self. Without it, the madness of our self-chosen current destructions, both personal and societal, saps the resources we may have thought we had. With this teaching at the core of our being, however, the energy and power which completes and is steadfast is not merely some further energy which we can conjure up after a good night's sleep, but rather a power which escapes our machinations yet which is present right within our own attempts at turning things around.

"He said to me, 'My grace is enough for you, for in weakness power reaches perfection.' And so I willingly boast of my weaknesses instead, that the power of Christ may rest upon me. Therefore I am content with weakness, with mistreatment, with distress, with persecutions and difficulties for the sake of Christ; for when I am powerless, it is then that I am strong" (1 Cor 12:9-10).

If anyone reads this scripture and uses it as an excuse for sauntering past life and involvement then the whole point of the teaching is lost. The word calls us to greater investment in our world and in our times. That we may feel puny about who we are will be no excuse for non-involvement or hiding in some dallying that we have the gall to call ministry. Paul is talking to people highly invested in life, people who are strong in their weakness because God has turned them around. God has indeed opened the eyes of the blind. We have moved inward to knowing the self. In that journey to weakness, we find power. It is with this power that the lame walk and the deaf hear. It is with this power that the reign of God is proclaimed.

CHAPTER THREE

Lice and Camels

The Spirit: "You will live among the sick in
great humility as long as I see fit
and do so without interruption"

Human Frailty: "I have tried one extreme and the
other. Better to endure these trials
than the fire of divine rays. Still,
one way and the other, both
frighten me."

Catherine of Genoa in
The Spiritual Dialogue

SO utterly did 15th-century Catherine Fieschi Adorno
of Genoa want to identify with the poorest and most unfortunate people in her town that she ate the lice that had
infested their bodies and their clothing. It is a shocking
story and one that makes us scorn pious hagiography
with more than the usual repulsion. The account repels,
but our repugnance might lead to some basic questions
about the manner of our churchly involvement with
"the poor."

We've always donated to the missions, to food pantries,
and to any of the multiple causes brought to our attention.
We grew up saving pagan babies; today, we give to "The
Children's Fund." In letters, popes and bishops have
called for help and we have responded. A priest from
Africa tells us, just as we arrived at church after a very
adequate dinner with the family, that his people often
have only bananas to eat. We quickly stuffed a few coins
or bills into the collection basket and acknowledge those

helpless guilts we felt when long ago our mothers urged us to clean our plates because the children in China (the country varies with the mother!) were starving. Today, a handful of Latin American persons, mostly lay women and men with a few bishops, theologians, and religious, are trying to shape Christian community structures around a preferential option for the poor. Their foundational thesis is that Jesus taught that God was mediated and accessible precisely in those whom the religious persons of the time thought were the riffraff of society—the ritually impure, lepers, aliens, sinners, outcasts, and anyone who didn't fit the mold of bourgeois religiosity. The religious folks were not merely to be charitable and polite to the dregs of society: Jesus insisted that the face of God in human history is impressed upon the *anawim*, the poor and humble who know their need for salvation and who cannot presume the power to save themselves. Rich people can usually feel much more omnipotent about life. Not only in Latin America but in every country in the world Christians are being called to examine their religious practice which in many instances has become too comfortable and too out of touch with the economically poor.

Catherine of Genoa was a competent and powerful woman who, by reason of her position of wealth and knowledge, had much influence over the local power structures. Lice became a possible means for her progress to solidarity with and compassion for others. Probably for this capable woman anything short of such an extraordinary and revolting action still smacked of personal control, manipulation of persons, and an altruistic service which carefully avoided the mutual relationships which healing and compassion demand. Capable people can so conveniently do their charities without becoming personally involved. Perhaps the lice are a detail stark enough to drive us past pious verbosity and useless guilt concerning the poor and oppressed of the world. The story might push more of the church community to some honest investigation of the poverty and stress around us in order to learn the meaning of presence and solidarity with suffering persons in other than theoretical or televised encounters. Instead of some vast anonymous horde called "the poor," we might become involved with people who influence and shape our lives.

Solidarity is a very popular word, and our red-and-white lapel buttons show our acceptance of a people's choice for justice through organization of the labor force. Being able to be in solidarity with another human being is, however, something dreadfully hard to do. Catherine of Genoa ate the lice. She had washed and cleaned, talked and cared, but she was still other. She had established adequate care facilities through pressuring influential people who were her acquaintances. She was still other deep within herself. The woman had an extraordinary insight and sensitivity for solidarity and real compassion. She knew she needed to become one with; anything short of a true solidarity was, for her, merely a comfortably orchestrated philanthropy. She forced herself to an action so repugnant to her bourgeois piety that breakthrough to solidarity became possible. Obviously, the story is not calling us to befriend lice-ridden persons in order to model solidarity. It tells us only that our complex of motivations for everything we do must be purified until our gestures of justice and charity are not based on self-gratification. Catherine had moved far beyond puny reasons for living her life the way she did. She had come through too much emotional illness, a terribly difficult marriage, even frail health. The account brings to mind other stories of persons who kissed lepers or who went among the plague-stricken without letting fear of contamination dominate their actions. What peculiar summons have all these people heard that brought them beyond a natural preference for safety and comfort to the possibility of solidarity and compassion?

Too many of us are so excessively preoccupied with our psychological and physiological ups and downs that we are light years away from that exquisite sensitivity to another that is the indication of the presence of solidarity and compassion. We know our astrological signs, our Chinese horoscopes, our Jungian proclivities, our Sufi characteristics and our biorhythms; with manuals in hand, we are able to account for our every psychic undulation. When Jupiter lies next to Mars, we know just why we're feeling the way we do. With this extraordinary introversion, it is no wonder that solidarity is well nigh impossible. We may read or talk about commitment to the oppressed of the world, but we can't even be in solidarity with the lady across the hall. Our self-centered conversations, our lack of hearing what another is saying, our body language of withdrawal—all indicate we have no notion whatever of how to walk in another's moccasins. We are caught up in a vortex of our individual absorptions. Knowing the self is helped by various psychotherapies certainly, but one can progress on the journey only by life experiences which have been sifted into God: The passage in and out of the storms, the movement toward reflective prayer, and the gradual ability for renunciation and self-denial about which the gospel speaks, a self-denial utterly different from the martyrologies we like to read off about ourselves.

The ability to establish solidarity begins when one undertakes the journey to the self. We will be in solidarity with another if we receive and accept our own weakness, powerlessness, and humanness apart from any of our various subterfuges. Knowing the self and thus being enabled to know another is the foundation of all wisdom. Lest this sentence sound like some cryptic message from Kung Fu's Master spoken against a background of wind chimes and soft-fluttering petals, it must be asserted that, without this truth as foundation, we will wander for years in and out of various causes but never be able really to make any impact upon our world. We are just one more person lost from self, able only to stand before others with unresolved angers, surface solutions, and unfelicitous cliches about their situations. However, we do not hide in our air-conditioned buildings waiting to gain enough compassion and solidarity to move outdoors into human history and mingle with the crowds. We mingle with the crowds and the crowds mingle with us while we're learning that oftentimes our liberalities are merely socially acceptable ways to wield control over others. To be with is the meaning of the solidarity we seek.

Another Catherine, this one from Siena, has offered us a further insight which aids our understanding of solidarity and compassion through the journey to the self. This Catherine determined that keeping the Ten Commandments was not an adequate spiritual path for the serious Christian. For the woman or man seeking a radical following of Jesus, the counsels of the gospel were the way: poverty, chastity, and obedience, three teachings or invitations that have been understood and misunderstood frequently in the history of the Christian community. Our experience has been that certain persons among the church faithful have vowed to live these counsels and the rest of us have blessed their choice while viewing ourselves exempted from such a lifestyle. Why do the words of this 14th-century Catherine have to turn up in the latter part of the 20th century to plague us with their challenge? She was a laywoman like her neighbor in Genoa. Why couldn't these Catherines accept their lot in life and not compound their troubles and ours by listening to the gospel? Why did they have to start getting peculiar about religion?

For wonderfully inexplicable and mysterious reasons both Catherines were utterly serious about following Jesus, and one of his counsels concerning discipleship was that of voluntary poverty. This teaching made them aware that just as camels have difficulty getting through the eyes of needles, so do rich people have difficulty proclaiming the reign of God since they have so much baggage to divert their attention from what really matters in this world. Scholars suggest that Needle's Eye was a particularly difficult mountain passage for camels to negotiate. In similar fashion, Jesus' followers are still confronted with negotiating a breakthrough from vague and comfortable religious attitudes to the single-minded vision of the Catherines.

There is a universal verity to the idea that we humans find satisfaction when we get what we want. At least we think we do. We learn very soon, however, that one wish or desire follows another in such rapid succession that we can recall walking out of a store with one pair of shoes we like and immediately being attracted to another pair we see in the window. The Buddha taught that all the sorrow of human life is in direct proportion to the cravings deeply resident in the heart of each individual. We think we are happiest when we have everything we desire; we go to any and all lengths to achieve possession only to find a new craving lurking around the corner from the old. The Buddha was certain that if one could get rid of craving, one could rid the world of sorrow. Easier said than done! We recognize that our cravings consume us unless we forcibly put a stop to them by such a thing as a vow of poverty.

The idea must be removed immediately from an association with the vow we know nuns take. They, too, are struggling anew with what the counsel means for them as are any serious Christians. The gospels are the basic scriptures for all those who claim to follow Jesus. To presume that there is one particular group in the church community who is to pay strict attention to what the gospel says, while others need not be bothered, is incredibly shortsighted. Monks and nuns have made a communitarian lifestyle work to their advantage. They put everything earned in the common fund and take from the common fund what is needed. Setting aside any religious dimension to these rules, they form a workable economic system which has guaranteed to most religious in the United States education, necessary travel and health care, in addition to adequate food and shelter. Most luxury items and the use of private properties have been relinquished, but, viewing the lunacy of a consumer and a throw-away society, the structures of a communal lifestyle are indeed sound if not in fact attractive. I do not dismiss cavalierly the serious gesture of public vows which some in the church have taken. Speaking as one from among them I can only attest that the counsels of the gospel are particular words of Jesus which each Christian has to listen to seriously each day. Those who have entered religious communities as the lifestyle in which they feel they can live out their Christian commitments are no exception. Neither are married persons nor those who have chosen not to marry. All of us are bound to the spiritual and the Christian journey. All of us have to figure out how to get through Needle's Eye.

The Spirit of God is bringing the entire church community into new and deeper understandings of the gospel message. Obviously this is the meaning of the renewal called for by Vatican II. Most of us are finished haranguing about the "changes" and are beginning to be able to deal realistically with the directions the Council pointed to. We are being summoned and changed, like it or not, by a power greater and more provident than ourselves. The gospel stands starkly in front of all of us for our comprehension, our acceptance and our action.

Voluntary poverty. Even the phrase sends chills into our shopping center hearts! Persons who for years have had a vow of poverty have begun, by the grace of God, to recognize that its interpretation lies well beyond the legal minimums that the Rules of congregations mandated. To be poor means ultimately to come before God stripped and naked of everything that has impeded the divine vision and its being lived out in daily practice. Everything we cling to that masks reality has to go, by choice and not by accident, if we are to perceive the dimensions of the reign of God in the present moment.

It is in the context of the reign of God that all life is to be lived. Jesus preached God's reign; he drew the symbol from a rich heritage in which God had acted to save, and these divine actions were identified in the ordinary daily experiences of the people. They were freed historically from oppressive rulers. God had rescued them. They were led to safety. God had acted. Food, land, and blessing were given; this abundance was God's doing. From the personal and communal recognition of God's active presence was drawn the symbol, the kingdom or reign of God. God reigned when peace, justice, and freedom happened within individuals and within societal relationships.

Jesus renewed the clarity and challenge of the insight: God was present and acting when the blind were seeing, the deaf hearing, the lame walking, and the poor receiving the gospel. His followers were to be intrinsically involved in God's activity, not in the sense that they made the kingdom come, but in that they were to view all of reality from this perspective and act as if they did. It would be one thing to request that followers teach Braille to the blind during one semester; it is quite another to make the demand that every aspect of one's life be focused into a single, directional vision. One semester is so much more manageable.

Moreover, though the reign of God carries with it an eschatological aspect, it is not utopian but practical and everyday. Wherever and however healing is happening, the reign of God is present. Don't look to the north or south, east or west, the kingdom is present in this moment if one has eyes to see and ears to hear. If external stimuli gathered by eyes and ears and recorded by the brain are interpreted superficially, then the mundane is the mundane and only and always that. But if one's optical and audial perceptions have been converted by faith, then daily events are interpreted into a totally different message.

We remonstrate: why do Jesus' followers have to see things differently? Why can't we be like those who have no faith? Why must we ascertain the presence of the reign of God within every external circumstance? We know of religious fanatics whose personal insecurities are so great that they are driven to pathological illusions of blessing and empowerment. How do we know that our convictions about the reign of God are not the pious dreams of world-weary misanthropes?

"I want to follow you."

"Go, sell what you have and give to the poor and then come follow me."

Jesus' mandate to his followers yesterday and today only complicates our devotional gestures. We are forced to examine the connection between this gospel counsel and the reign of God which is like the mustard seed, so small and imperceptible that we usually overlook its presence and its power. Jesus indicates that we might notice the reign of God actively occurring in our midst if we weren't so busy clinging to our possessions.

In a country where items which are a luxury to most of the world's peoples are cheaply available, where we have running water, electricity and vast resources of land and food, how can we live a gospel that counsels voluntary poverty? Even those who took a vow of poverty have money to have their teeth fixed and have hospital insurance. If they can't carry off the counsel then who can?

When we hear this gospel advice and confront the internal dilemma it creates, we give more money to Mother Teresa and persons like her who seem able to be and do what we cannot. Donate some money, and the saint can be on her way traveling about the world, caring for various children as photographers wire the images into our living rooms. We can't do what she does; we have neither the money nor the entree to people and places of wealth and importance. We live in particular neighborhoods with our families. Mobility is out of the question. We are priests whose parishes are bound into diocesan geographical boundaries. We are single young women or men struggling for a degree which we feel holds the key to our happiness and purposiveness in some future job. We are sisters or brothers in a religious community bound to one another and to our apostolic commitments. We have three cheap radios, and we have just purchased a new living room rug. We have even given the old one to the Salvation Army. What more?

This stream of consciousness haunts every serious follower of Jesus as well as many others who are not Christians. There is no other way to go through Needle's Eye now except with the living room rug strapped firmly to our backs. We have to squeeze through with the root canals we've had done, with our dogfood and wristwatches until that day comes when voluntary poverty and its realistic possibilities for each of us in our own lifestyle is in fact voluntary, that is, free and freeing.

Until our choices for less and not more are free and not compulsive and guilt-ridden, the call to sell what we have will strike at the core of each one's particular neurosis described in these scenarios: I am already 20 pounds overweight, and I am purchasing yet another half-gallon of ice cream. Many of the world's children are hungry. I eat the ice-cream; I am already too fat and others are starving. I am angry with myself and guilt-ridden in a useless welter of emotions. I buy another shirt knowing how many men and women are unemployed. I feel bad about it but never bad enough not to buy the shirt. I love electrical gadgets and my home already looks like the inside of a NASA station, but I find a new kind of calculator that will help me get my work done much faster. Guilt dogs my heels, but I've learned I forget its naggings after a while. I record TV programs while I'm asleep. I have access to computers which send collated and stapled pages of reports across the country in minutes. These scenarios, or similar ones of our own choosing, portray each of us. All humans have particular cravings, thus no design for voluntary poverty can be outlined which is applicable for all. But the gospel counsel stands: Sell what you have. Get through the needle's eye. Voluntary. Free. What can it mean?

All of us followers of Jesus, in whatever lifestyle—married, single, religious community, or clerical—have to deal with the gospel counsel, not by selling the living room rug through some misguided guilt, but because freely we choose to move toward a radical following of Jesus. Our choice may lead us to certain relinquishments as the years go along, but the prior relinquishment is leaving behind any and all obstacles, internal or external, that prevent the journey to the self.

How can all of these ideas fit together—the journey to the self and into God, the reign of God, compassion, solidarity, social change, voluntary poverty, gospel counsels, lice, and camels? They do. They are interconnected within the mystery of God's power known in our weakness. The choice to bring our lives into focus with Jesus' teaching about the reign of God stems directly from the degree to which we have undertaken the journey to the self. If we live on the periphery of our own reality, then we will be giving monetary donations to Mother Teresa into old age and feeling guilty about our personal

inabilities at compassion and solidarity. It is so difficult
for contented, comfortable church people in the United
States to learn the lesson of weakness. Our national instincts are for power, control, and social change through
our techniques and skills. Powerful people can know the
Crucified only by knowing their own weakness and
powerlessness; then only do we stand effectively by the
pain and sorrow of another. If we grapple with our weakness and confront our lack of godliness free from pious
pretense, we learn a genuine compassion which is no
longer a thinly disguised ruse to make everything turn out
our way. When we are overwhelmed by our weakness and
powerlessness over human pain which we cannot change,
overcome, or even assuage, then we identify with Jesus
crucified and call out in the same poverty: "My God, my
God, why have you abandoned us?"

It is then we gain the meaning of the eschatological
aspect of the reign of God. We have learned that the reign
of God is a present reality, yet it will not be completed
until God is all in all. Seeing the kingdom of God in the
present moment depends on our faith to perceive God
present in daily situations and on our choices to dedicate
our days to the happening of the kingdom. But when we
come up against utter powerlessness in ourselves, in
other's lives and in the vast extent of global injustice—it
is then we understand what theologians call the eschatological dimension of the reign of God. We used to
interpret this teaching as the heavenly promise that all
unjust situations would be ultimately rectified: wicked
persons would get punished, and those who had been
downtrodden would get a better mansion than the rich
now located in a little shack on the other side of the
ethereal tracks. But eschatological refers to the "not-yet"

kingdom in the sense that it symbolizes the hopes and dreams for world peace and justice deep within all our hearts. The reign of God which is yet to be fully realized is the accumulation of all the dreams in the hearts of people that continue to bring about social change. We have known change for good to occur historically, and thus we have reason to hope. We cling to our dreams and do everything we can do to make them come true. Justice fails and injustice prevails in the now; our hopes and dreams urge us forward to the reign of God which is not yet all in all. The alternative is cynicism and despair, both of which lead to a deep-seated frustration with the futility of mortal existence. Love and choices for hope and love make a difference. In simple language, the kingdom of God is our loving and being loved, and the eschatological kingdom is our search and work for the possibility for life and love for all humanity. Then indeed is God all in all.

Lice taught Catherine of Genoa that she had a long way to go to become the woman of compassion she wanted to be, and camels teach all of us that squeezing through narrow places burdened with excess baggage requires immense psychic energy that might better be spent in the pursuit of self-possession and self-knowledge. We might better provide and accept love and happiness in the brief days we spend on planet Earth and open our minds and our lives to our global brothers and sisters.

Needle's Eye offers a particular richness. It behooves us to search out the freedom that lies on the other side. The honest journey to self-knowledge allows us to cast off a lot of baggage. God will occasion many possibilities to be truly poor in spirit and stripped of our deceits if we don't strap on all our trappings, tightly buttressing up a self-image based on pathetic little or great deceptions. We pray to be led beyond the limitations of our own trivial machinations. We will be. God knows better than we about needles and camels and even, of course, about the lice.

CHAPTER FOUR

Sheep and Wolves

"What I am doing is sending you out like sheep among wolves. You must be clever as serpents and innocent as doves.... You will be brought to trial before rulers and kings, to give witness before them and before the Gentiles on my account."

Jesus in Matthew 10

JESUS did not preach himself. He proclaimed that God must reign over all the earth, a reign completed when all afflicted persons would be healed and all oppressive situations changed. In Jesus' proclamation lay the hopes and dreams of his ancestors that a different world could eventually be theirs. Justice, peace, and freedom would characterize both societal and personal relationships. The establishment of God's rule was to happen in the present; fulfillment would be in the end times, but the hour of God's action was always the now. The signs of the Presence were self-revelatory: the blind saw, the deaf heard, the lame walked, and the poor received the Good News of salvation. All humanity was blind and poor and the changes and conversions were evident to faith.

Since the time of Jesus, women and men in all life-styles—named variously by the church as disciples, missionaries, apostles, and ministers—have given their lives over to the extension of the work of Jesus in multiple ways. The commitment did not change the practical details of day-to-day work, family or community involvements, but it very definitely undergirded the worldview of the person who by grace felt somehow compelled to give energy over to the works of God.

We followers of Jesus know that the summons to proclaim the reign of God and 'to heal the afflicted forms the center to which our total life-story is connected. Sheep among wolves indeed! The perpetrators of sinful social structures call us naive for the dreams we envision about a different kind of world. These dreams are not the frail illusions of simpletons but the hard-won convictions of serious human beings who refuse to accept sin, greed, and deceit as the content of human relationships. Through all the centuries, though often uncertain or inarticulate about their initial summons, women and men joined the ranks of their predecessors in the faith who knew that religion was somehow a peculiar madness if it did not involve the love and service of others.

In the gospels we witness Jesus as a master teacher of disciples. He led his followers through successive stages of spiritual growth as they matured into the leaders who could extend the salvation of God to all the earth. We read about an initial summons followed only sometime later by specific instructions that the vocation is for the reign of God. The call would eventually lead to a ife so like that of Jesus, that the disciple was to become another Jesus. This identification with Jesus was a fulfillment fraught with the weariness, commitment, and the eventual death which Jesus knew, yet blessed with the transformations, the life, and the glory which was the promise of God to those who in baptism freely chose to become daughters and sons of God. Jesus had no illusions about the situations his disciples would meet as they started out to preach and heal. Though these early followers probably presumed that they had tied their wagons to a rising star, they soon learned that conflict surrounded their leader and that Jesus was a figure of contradiction.

The path to self-knowledge through ministerial responsibility is one illumined with early hopes and dreams, yet one which contains a gradually developing weariness over our miscalculations about the whole enterprise. It can culminate in the formation, by God's power, of the woman or man who will be a ready instrument for justice. Jesus knew that one's process to becoming disciple consisted of certain non-negotiable components. If the life-experience of particular individuals exposed them to specific occurrences through which they had to make their way, then just possibly, by the right combination of nature and grace, a disciple was being readied for the following of Jesus. It takes us long years to gain the craft of the serpent while yet retaining the pure intent of the dove. When confronted with the deceits, machinations, and downright ignorance inside oneself, as well as inside and outside the churches and civic communities, most disciples would simply like to run for cover and no longer call upon any internal powers to jump into the breaches of confrontation, argument, and serpentine decisions. Yet, if beginners allow it and do not falter, the Spirit of Jesus makes disciples of us even now.

For many years the Holy Spirit has been leading the church to a very specific self-understanding: the church is nothing more and nothing less than the gathering of those who are disciples of Jesus. Discipleship, with all the word denotes, is the fundamental identity for the Christian. To be disciple is a role with a definite, daily practice connected to its faith. Faith offers a meaning structure for all of life, but one that is fruitless unless it shapes everyday attitudes and actions in particular ways.

The formation of a disciple was one of Jesus' most requiring tasks. Today it is the Spirit of God who forms disciples through some of the very same life-processes we witness in the stories of the first apostles. One of the educative needs for the woman or man who would be disciple is engagement in ministerial works. The beginning disciple needs to be involved in works of service to the neighbor. In recent church history this call by the Holy Spirit to active ministerial responsibility has been given various names. In the forties the phrase "lay apostle" came into vogue; we were allowed and directed to participate in the apostolic work of the hierarchy. Today we recognize the inadequacy of that insight as we have learned that our mission is directly connected with the purport of our baptisms. Ministry constitutes an essential part of the life of the follower of Jesus.

I choose not to quibble with the names and designations we've been given through the years or ought to be given now. What is important is that each of us identify the action of the Spirit historically present in the various ecclesial pronouncements and recognize the logical outcome: we who claim to be followers of Jesus are, by the fact of our baptisms, irrevocably bound into the redemptive work of Jesus. Our lives have significance only in one context: that God reign as all in all. In very simple terms this means that the blind will see, the deaf hear, and the poor learn of the gospel. Our lives are about identifying these continuous graced interventions of God in our personal and corporate histories.

It seems that this interior comprehension of our mission is the highest mysticism. To those who are suspicious of that theology we call "political," one can only dispute the significance of a piety or reverence that is totally unconnected to daily events. When the faithful individual, however, in an overwhelming conversion understands that religious and daily life are, must be, and only can be one reality, then a proper mysticism is alive on this earth. God has again been kind to us and blessed us with persons of integrity for whom the vision of the reign of God has come into a single focus with the details of daily life. Mystics are those wonderful people who so amazingly see reality in a single focus despite ambiguity, doubt, fear of failure, and daily frustrations.

Catherine of Genoa was one of these. As we know, she was a remarkably competent and powerful woman who had come through years of emotional conflict, relational struggles, and near madness, to integrity, vision, and utter commitment to the gospel of Jesus. Until his conversion, her husband was nothing but a wanton philanderer. The final years of her life as administrator, humanitarian, spiritual guide to men and women, and her total and preferential option for the poor reveal Catherine to us as someone to know.

That she died in 1510 notifies us that she lived in the shadow of a terribly corrupt church, yet here was an extraordinary woman whose personal religious experience was so profound that it freed her from excessive dependence on authority, pious structures, or religious legalities. She was God's daughter; hers was a love that was of the life of God, itself Love. From this base she faced her times without faintheartedness and with an amazing assurance that her insights and dreams were accurate. How wonderful to know focus when all around is blurred and confused! This woman knew the will of God in the daily occurrences of one incident after another. Nothing spectacular, simply the purgations that brought one to knowing what love is all about. A stern lesson this. Shouldn't loving be painless? Why does it take so much from us? Why do we need so much purifying to learn how to love? Only the adolescents among us don't suspect the answers to those questions.

Catherine was a political woman, that is, her piety was rooted strongly in and among the people. The path to God was not around or away from the people. Hers was not a separate existence within the mind's cloister. This woman lived at the heart of her times and at the pace of her century. Think what it took for her and her husband to make the decision to relinquish their home and go to live in a few small rooms at the hospital in which she was administrator. This is not a lesson to us to abandon home but a call to abandon anything that prevents our following Jesus. The prudential judgments and decisions that precede actions are warp and woof of who we understand ourselves to be and of who we are becoming.

The story of Catherine Adorna gives us the outline of an applied political theology. A political theology suggests basically no more than taking at their full value and import the two greatest commandments. We are to love God with an entirety of mind, soul, body, and strength and to love our neighbor as ourselves. The more illusory and self-serving the first becomes, the more vapid is the latter. Once both commandments electrify a woman or man, the impossibility of conniving on either one becomes evident. Thus a political theology is defined in the words of another Catherine, this one with the surname Benincasa from Siena, to whom God says: "The only way to love me or to do service to me is to love your neighbor."

Thus, one of the major elements constitutive of the Christian's journey to the self is involvement in the mission of Jesus. Many books have been written about ministry, and there is no need to duplicate their messages. The only point to make here is that an apostolic life is essential to the formation of the follower of Jesus. It is crucial to a disciple's maturation that there be time, thought, and effort given to service of the neighbor. Jesus recognized well the human need to do something worthwhile and to interact with people toward some humanly valuable purposes. An evidence of Jesus' ability as master teacher was his recognition that it is precisely in the work of ministering in various ways that the disciples would face their own confusions, begin to deal with the complexity of the problems which surround human service and interaction, and admit that Jesus is a conflictual figure whose message summons humankind to a totally different understanding of what living life is all about.

Oddly enough, as we reach out to be with and for others, we discover who we are and how we are on a journey to God. A false dilemma is constructed between the self-journey and ministerial involvement. The two are in fact one coherent event of our evolving maturation. If anything, the mission to which Jesus' disciples are called exists so that all people can undertake the journey to the face of God who is revealed to them through the countenances of the disciples.

As a beginner approaches ministerial responsibility, the demeanor is one of confidence in one's abilities to get the job done. There is a natural zest for worthwhile commitment coupled with a high degree of desire to imitate Jesus in doing some good upon this earth. Given our citizenship, we attack a ministry the way we set out to conclude a business deal, clean the garage, or hang the new drapes. Get the job done. Measure the task. Plan the strategies and do it. There is nothing we can't do if we know how to go about it. Given the sincerity of the desire, immense energies seem available for the tasks ahead. The definition of ministry as "doing for" is enticing and captivates those whose needs to be needed impel them into ministry. It's easier to "do for" than to let oneself become part of the often tangled, complex, and sometimes broken skeins of relationships which true ministry entails. The amateur disciple soon learns, however, that "helping others" is not what ministry, apostolate, or discipleship is all about.

Ministry involves a series of relationships and a mutuality among all the participants in the action. As soon as there are persons in our lives who are not to be "done for" but rather are persons who mutually give and take, then we ministers see ourselves involved in an entirely different enterprise from what we had at first presumed. To shovel the snow for Mrs. McGillicudy is a much more involved gesture than we had ever presumed. It would be so much easier if we could just do something for someone and then go away. Why does God's reign involve relationships and dealings with the troubled aspects of ourselves and others?

The persons who surround my life are not there to be acted upon but to be interacted with. The interaction forces us disciples to live differently. Ministry understood in this way suggests all the pain and struggle that occur as well as all the joys, complications, misunderstandings, losses, hirings and firings, new beginnings, and new directions. The ministers begin to see themselves in totally new dimensions. Discipleship is more complex than we had ever presumed. That the blind must see is immediately broadened in our understanding to include our closest comrades and even ourselves. The changes consequent in us because of difficult situations lead eventually to our acting out in our lives what Jesus had accomplished in his. Jesus had to preach the God he uniquely and supremely knew over against the god which the religious leaders of his time had carved in their own image. The course upon which Jesus set his feet led to charges of blasphemy and ultimately to his murder. The disciples are to do and to be no less. The apostle of Jesus is another Jesus. We see this identification happen in the lives of the early followers of Jesus as they were captured and killed by the forces of evil which resisted the advancement of the reign of God.

We cannot expect anything less for ourselves as disciples and ministers today. We are to respond to the initial call; we are to be open to the instructions with which the Spirit of God surrounds our lives; we are to enter into ministry in order that through all of its circumstances we are refined and honed into instruments for salvation. The ways in which ministers are brought to courts and synagogues for trial today are somewhat more urbane than in Jesus' day. Today when we speak out against nuclear arms, when we demand that oppressive governments regard human rights, when we insist that women be given equal rights before the law, we are called naive dupes of the communists or persons who threaten the stability of the family. Bishops and religious types are to remain devoutly in their cathedrals while the financiers and worldly-wise masterminds dictate national policy. What possible wisdom can piety bring to the ship of state? Thus are the disciples of Jesus called into question today. At one time the only aggravation the civic community received from churches were the bells awakening the neighborhood too early on worship mornings. Now the awakenings are of a different sort, and worldly powers have their subtle ploys lined up against the people of religious conviction who attempt to speak to national policy.

The disciple is to be another Jesus. What an extraordinary claim! Being faithful over many years to the endless details of a ministerial life will demand of us a courage and a faith rooted only in the grace and power of God. Why did Jesus choose to lead his disciples through such a morass of tangled emotions, dedications, and waning energies? Why does the Spirit of God today lead disciples through the same processes of ministerial conflict and responsibility? Catherine of Siena offers us a hint to the answer: "So that you will come to know yourself." How odd! One would think it would be because we have to come to know what others are like or that we would get to know more about God and about the enterprises of God in which we are involved. To come to know ourselves. How seemingly trivial a task over against the gigantic ministerial possibilities of today. Yet without our ministries being founded in this journey to identification with Jesus, our enterprises end in misguided ego trips and multiple examples of foolhardy and wasted energy. The complexity and confusion of the ministerial life can lead us to knowledge of ourselves and primarily, of course, to the divine intent: that we experience the weakness of humanity into which the power of divinity has entered. God's power is made known in our weakness. We know our weakness ever more clearly as we face the responsibilities of the ministerial life.

In understanding the religious activities of church people in this way, we do not place as a first goal our own human development while neglecting or placing second the needs of our world, particularly any sinful social structures whether ecclesial or societal which must be challenged. An integrity between making the journey to self-knowledge and dedicating time and energy to ministry is the only viable Christian stance. The disciple who is consumed with unidentifiable childhood angers or who is battling personal demons will need immense purification before the gospel can be heard through the rage. It may seem that a given individual combats every evildoer or evil situation from a storehouse of righteousness and zeal, but we learn one day that some fierce doomsayers were really never disciples but merely warmongers in religious guises. Should these lines comfort the sedentary among us, we must admit before God that undertaking the rigor of a ministerial life is incumbent upon all of us. It is filled with dangerous pitfalls and is the most wonderful and challenging possibility for the followers of Jesus. All our pretenses and illusions about ourselves as good and well-meaning folks will get burned away until our own phoenixes of truth and authenticity can rise from the ashes of our grandiose and righteous postures. Unresolved angers may seem to generate endless dynamism, but the disciple must be brought by God's grace beyond sporadic and shrill forays into ministry. Day-to-day fidelity and commitment are independent of personal whim. We know we can no longer deceive ourselves about the kind of ministerial effort we undertake. It will do no good for a competent and powerful businessman to ladle soup twice annually to the hungry and dispossessed. Somehow this man must utilize the gifts and talents of mind, heart, and body to figure out why people are hungry and dispossessed and do whatever is possible

to change systems which prolong and guarantee injustice. Nor can an equally powerful and competent, well-
educated woman content herself with ironing the altar
cloths for Christmas. The point here is not the value and
merit of ladling soup or ironing but rather the recognition
of a total lifestyle based on who and what we are that is
to be given over to the reign of God and the healing of the
afflicted in ways that affect the social structures that
perpetuate evil. Working to change unjust social systems
is a very complex ministry. Many persons have presently
undertaken the task and recognize that ministry here too
consists of dealing with the skeins of tangled relationships
and ferreting out the ill-formed ideas which keep the
blind, blind, and the poor, poor. The trouble with social
sin is that no one individual is personally responsible for
the evil; all of us are intricately and inextricably involved.
Thus the tangled skeins are here even more tangled.

Each follower of Jesus according to her and his gifts
and talents must evaluate frequently their efforts toward
the happening of the kingdom. Some have had to change
jobs; some have had to move either geographically or in
their heads. All have had to recognize that the redemptive
mission of Jesus, incumbent upon us, demands a 24-hour
commitment. There is a need to separate linguistically
what we do to earn a living, which obviously is filled with
missionary possibilities, from our commitment to
discipleship, which consumes the entirety of our lives.
For example, Catholic sisters cannot feel their ministry
is over when they go home from work at the hospital, law
office, or parish. Permanent deacons cannot refer to what
they do in their off-hours in hospice, nursing home, or
kindergarten as ministry while the other hours of a week
are nonministerial. Faithful parishioners cannot separate

their daily humane decisions and practices from their sense of what church is all about. Priests and retired persons are never free from the mission of Jesus that proclaims God and heals a world. Vacations and days off may be days away from the job; none of us is ever away from mission. This sentence is rendered absurd if we imagine that disciples go about wide-eyed, searching for openings in conversations in order to speak a religious sentence. Enough novels have portrayed this pathetic and threadbare sort of minister. But that the follower of Jesus can never forget what following is about is the point at issue. The crazy summons burns away at our pretenses, our excuses, and our vague religiosity. The entire content of the lives of the followers of Jesus must be focused with the ongoing happening of the kingdom of God. This means that the eye of faith is alert and ready to identify the kingdom at all times and that God-given and God-impelled energies which are beyond natural zest are steadily employed so that the blind will see, the deaf hear, and the poor know the Good News.

Practically speaking, the vision obviously eventuates in shoveling the snow, running the political campaign, picketing, or ladling the soup. But the heart-vision is constant and the comprehension of what it means to meet other people, to know them, to become involved with them, to listen, to grow, to change, to fail, to succeed, to learn, to change, to draft plans, to be irritated, to be angry, to change, to mellow, to become wise, to be crucified, to rise again, to change—all through many years—is what a life of ministry is all about. It is the journey to the self, the journey to the neighbor, and the journey into God simultaneously.

There is a caution which merits attention. We can only

hope, given the contemporary stress placed on the laity
in ministry, that what has been written here will enable
us to be clear about the call. There is a danger that certain
rhetoric translates into giving one hour a week at the
nursing home rather than into comprehending that the
entirety of one's life is missionary. The value of the one
hour a week at the nursing home is the value of exposure
to ways of life that are outside our insular and predictable
lifestyles. The possibilities for awakening and for new
commitments to following Jesus which might result from
our growing insights into the meaning of human
diminishment are vast. The one hour a week can perhaps
provide the possibility for solidarity and compassion. It
is with this hope that the call is given. But it is when we
and the men and women at the nursing home *meet*, that
the mutuality that ministry implies becomes operative.

Only as life chips away at our personal intransigencies
do we become women or men who are being gotten ready
by the power of God for leadership. In the leader-disciple
one recognizes the gift for justice, unflagging and steadfast, that is given to the church. Here is a person that the
oppressors of society need to fear because this person will
never quit.

The mission of Jesus can be clearly stated; the possibilities for ministries involved in the extension of God's
reign are multiple. Our choice of ministry arises from a
prayerful discernment of our gifts and an assessment
within the community group of the signs of the times
which make the saving mission of Jesus a present reality.
I have read that when an avalanche occurs, there are those
persons who hand out coffee to the survivors; there are
those who begin the task of clearing the road; and there
are those who try to figure out why the avalanche happened and work to prevent its occurring again. These

three kinds of involvement in specific ministerial works are chosen by disciples of Jesus today. The community of disciples, the church, summons those among us who have the skills to work at changing the systems which create the avalanches of social injustices and oppressions in our world. Others among us hand out the food and clothing and some are busy clearing all the kinds of debris that social injustice leaves in its wake. The particular ministry into which disciples enter puts us in "this" place with "these" people to deal with "these relationships" which are the localized ministry. There will be headaches and disappointments. There are failures and successes. But the kingdom, like the mustard seed, is perceptible to the eye which sees reality now in a different context than it did formerly. Sheep and wolves. Jesus was not exaggerating, and the disciple cannot underestimate or misjudge the power of the preying animal. But the power that enters the disciple is a power beyond muscle and brain. It is a power that for centuries has moved faithful persons beyond their native capabilities to possibilities for self-gift, generosity, and magnanimity beyond puny, personal resources. We have sailed the seas, we have endured torture, we have marched against the oppressors. The followers of the crucified God have not necessarily been giants personally. But a power has carried them to self-transcendence. The neighbor has been loved. The blind have seen. Human limitations and smallness of vision were surpassed. Bunglers in ecclesiastical and civic positions were outwitted. The reign of God has continued to extend itself into the hearts and minds of humankind. Disciples stand mutely in awe of a power outside themselves, a power salvific, a power tangible and intangible, a power crucified, a power risen.

CHAPTER FIVE

Unicorns and Rhinoceroses

With downcast eyes, not loitering
With guarded senses, warded thoughts,
With mind that festers not, nor burns,
Fare lonely as rhinoceros.

And turn thy back on joys and pains,
Delights and sorrows known of old;
And gaining poise and calm and cleansed
Fare lonely as rhinoceros.

Astir to win the yondmost goal
Not lax in thought, nor sloth in ways
Strong in the onset, steadfast, firm,
Fare lonely as rhinoceros.

Like lion fearful not of sounds,
Like wind not caught within a net,
Like lotus not by water soiled,
Fare lonely as rhinoceros.

From the *Sutta Nipata*

AMONG the many difficult human goals, one of the more arduous is to become single-hearted. We are only too well aware of the complex motivations and muddied reasons that cling to our every act. To rid a deed of its knotted skeins of intention seems an impossible and perhaps useless pursuit. Besides, why opt for purity of intent or purpose? The anecdote of the rider mounting a horse and riding off in all directions captures well the patterns to which we've become accustomed and often

70

those which we prefer. Constant movement allows us to feel engaged in worthwhile efforts and projects. We pretend we haven't time to undertake the journey to the self. Searching out our motives, and this with some honesty, demands a personal truth we like to avoid. My contention is that Jesus' teaching about being a eunuch for the kingdom of God, unless one chooses to interpret eunuch in its literal sense, is a summons to a profound singleness of heart for all serious Christians. Matthew 19 records the statement:

> It is not everyone who can accept what I have said, but only those to whom it is granted. There are eunuchs born that way from their mother's womb, there are eunuchs made so by men, and there ae eunuchs who have made themselves that way for the sake of the kingdom of heaven. Let anyone accept this who can.

If read in the literal sense, which we church people have seldom done except for an occasional Origen, one-half of the Christian population is immediately deprived of the possibility of carrying out the counsel: women simply can't be eunuchs. Lest church historians and biblical scholars rise up with exegetical dismay, let me say only that I wish not to enter the lists of textual criticism. I prefer to think beyond the traditionally accepted interpretation of the passage which centers on marrying or not marrying, and to lay stress on the phrase "for the kingdom of God." This decision is not necessarily part of the debate for or against optional celibacy but rather a reflection focused by unicorns and rhinoceroses as these creaturely sisters and brothers indicate to us something about single-heartedness.

For Christians the unicorn has symbolized solitary purposiveness and a clear-eyed chastity in the fullest sense of the word. The mythical beast has been used to represent Jesus who, with a perfect unity of being and singleness of vision, sought and carried out the divine intent. In many legends the strange animal was never captured except by the woman, a remarkable phantasy suggesting that single-heartedness is a desire of each man or woman, deep and inexplicable yet known and experienced by the feminine in us. Especially when present complexities threaten to choke our unfathomable yearnings for simplicity are we aware of that aspect of our psyches signified by the unicorn. Buddhists have expressed the same insight through the character of the rhinoceros. This thick-skinned mammal possesses one or two upright horns which appear to point in a single direction; it does not run with the herd and thus "fares lonely."

The rhinoceros and the unicorn have imparted their single wisdom to artists through the centuries to enable them to point to that longing in the human heart for single directions and purposes over against a random scattering of energy with no real loves or commitments nor any steady determinations or involvements. All of us distrust the perpetual commuter personality. The pathos of constantly commuting among multiple pathways allows the feel of journeying, but the movement is outward only and self-discovery has not been begun. Futility jostles our tedious complacencies. To what purposes and to whom am I committed and for what reasons?

If, in our consideration of the real and mythical animals, we lay stress on whether or not they couple, the power of the symbol wanes. There is obviously some other dimension more compelling about their physiology than an asexuality freely chosen or enforced. Taking a broad leap, I suggest that the gospel counsel to be eunuch for the kingdom of God has significance beyond sexual interpretations, that is, beyond the translations of marrying or not marrying, beyond the impossibiity of women eunuchs, and beyond the aberrations of castration stories. It is a counsel that enlightens those with clean hearts, the seers of God. The counsel has been a summons through the centuries far broader than our religious circumferences have admitted.

The fundamental question is whether the counsels of the gospel are for all Christians or just for a few elite individuals. Though it is obvious that we have heeded them in practice more or less well, the counsels were given to all of us. In the 14th century Catherine of Siena insisted that being serious about following Jesus included a great deal more than rigidly keeping the Ten Commandments. Those believers concerned about discipleship would have to do something about getting through the eyes of needles, about being eunuchs for the kingdom, and about becoming obedient even to death on the cross. Now before the fainthearted among us draw back from the challenge, and before the passers-of-the-buck concede responsibility for the gospel to monks and nuns, we should assess what is happening among us church people in the extraordinary times in which we find ourselves.

We are a church come of age who are moving beyond the memorized responses and replies of our corporate adolescence. Within us is a mysterious, indistinct yet evident summons to a new paradigm of what it means to follow Jesus. The patent leather shoes and white tablecloths (if in fact they ever possessed any significance) have lost any prurience to attract the man or woman who has undertaken the journey to a personal spirituality grounded in knowing the self. That this journey has been undertaken simply means we've asked a question of life's pretenses: "is this all there is?" We've answered, "no" and have proceeded along an enigmatic, divine roadway somewhat haltingly, challenging our religious tradition and demanding from its depths the richness of its wisdom. Many of us have finally ascertained that the rules and regulations, instead of being the totality of the dispensation of faith, are the results of Jesus' and his followers religious insights. With these, wayfarers like ourselves could be brought by God's power to the expeience of salvation in our present history as well as to an assurance of an eternal presence in the communion of saints.

For a long time we have been content to relegate "eunuch-hood" to vowed religious and priests. If these persons somehow felt called to give up marriage and family for God and the church, then blessings upon them. The others among us would people the earth and work by the sweat of our brows. There have always been the Marys and the Marthas. Let the celibates and eunuchs be Mary; the others among us would have to grapple with the practical realities.

Can we recall when it became evident to us that simply not being married was no guarantor at all of seeking God with a single heart? Somewhere in the last twenty years of our religious history when various walls, doors, and windows of churches, convents, and monasteries were opened, the Catholic faithful met one another across the lines of our chosen lifestyles. We learned that there were single-hearted nuns and mothers; there were single-hearted TV repair persons and priests, and, oddly enough, it began to dawn on us that there were other mothers, bishops, and bakery clerks who in fact had never made any adult choices toward seeking the face of God with any singleness of purpose at all.

At first we were afraid to think such thoughts. That the pastor tippled a little too much was a fact we parishioners had trained ourselves to wink at, but that among the celibates were all the sins that humankind has named was an unthinkable thought. Surely the dark side of humanity could not be predicated of the eunuchs for the kingdom. Sadly, we recognized the pathetic fact. Some among the eunuchs were only that—eunuchs. The "for the kingdom" aspect had somehow slipped away from their consciousness if it had ever been there at all. We had to look for the real eunuchs by starting at the other end of the phrase. Whenever we came upon men or women filled with a single-hearted urgency that God's reign of justice, peace, and freedom happen in every person and in every societal relationship, we knew we had found a real eunuch. Oddly enough, these real ones were in all walks of life. There were some overwhelmingly holy and wise Catholic sisters, married men, and archbishops who had indeed captured the essence of the gospel counsel.

Many churchgoers are dismayed by such an egalitarian leveling of the faithful. Only grudgingly can we think the possibility of very single-hearted human beings whose eunuch-hood is lived out quite well in the context of married life. Some of us still refuse to take communion from the unordained and weave our way through the church aisles in search of the anointed hand. Some among the clergy and religious do not like to see eunuch broadly defined because the definition forces them be-

yond mere sexual renunciations to an urgency that the
kingdom come. Religious position, prestige, and
prominence are hard to let go. "Look at all we've given up.
Surely all Catholics can't achieve in holiness what a
celibate can achieve, can they?" The answer is very simply
a resounding "yes." There is no particular mystique about
a celibate existence except that for some among the followers of Jesus it is their chosen lifestyle and it is indeed
their way to God.

Vocation can no longer be defined in the sexual categories of married, religious, or single states. One questions
why we were ever content to employ the lifestyle in which
people found themselves happiest as definition for vocation. The vocation of the Christian is to the following of
Jesus. There is no question but that women and men in all
lifestyles are more or less committed to this discipleship.
Some Christians marry. Some become priests. Some
choose to be celibate. Except for those who merely wake
up one day in one lifestyle or the other, experience indicates that, with the deliberation and choice possible to
late adolescence, people determine that their happiness as
human beings lies in a particular lifestyle. Recall de
Lubac's definition of happiness: that state in women and
men that is present when our spiritual energies are functioning at their maximum. Recall also Aquinas' understanding that happiness is the goal for humankind. For
mysterious reasons in God's providence, we find our way
into a particular lifestyle, there to face the joys and
sorrows inherent in every day. No life choice or relationship is fortress against foolishness and error.

Each of us has the human taks of relationship/love and
freedom/detachment to accomplish. If we visualize these
in two columns, one of them would list the issues of rela-

tionship: responsibility, intimacy, love, friendship, sexual involvement, and all their ramifications. The second column must contain the tasks of freedom: liberation of heart, solitude, psychological independence, and detachment. Both columns pertain to those human labors for which each of us, in whatever lifestyle, is responsible. No celibate can neglect the tasks of loving and no married individual can forego the works of freedom. Our human maturation permeated by divine grace, thus our holiness, is dependent upon confronting and embracing the dual issues of loving and of being free. The human being moving to integrity is the one who resolves the ambiguities of the two in the center of the self into one lifestyle. The journey to the self depends utterly upon the accomplishment of these tasks. Like pendulums, we swing back and forth for years. To come to rest in a middle place perfectly balanced between love and freedom is one of the most difficult of human endeavors.

Yet out of the integrity of our loving and our liberation comes the possibility for the single-heartedness which the gospel counsels. There is no religious posture which can circumvent human maturation. Anything short of authentic singleness of purpose betrays itself in so many revealing ways. One recalls the anecdotes of Mass or novena attendees who name all the neighbors present or not present at the service. Only the raconteurs themselves seemed oblivious to the awkward self-manifestation.

The mystics of our tradition, known and unknown, and from all lifestyles comprehended the divine invitation which led them to an extraordinary singleness of purpose. They started out from all social classes, from all levels of formal and life-education, from mental health and mental illness, and suddenly found by God's grace that

their lives were becoming focused into a single vision.
They were as human beings defined within the context of
the kingdom of God. God must reign. God must be all in
all. This single insight became the structuring vision of
their days. They still washed pots and pans, changed the
tires on the car, read extensively or listened to great music,
but as the years went along all their experiences were
moving to a point of convergence. For the follower of
Jesus, life is about the reign of God. The blind must see,
the deaf must hear, and the lame walk. We and all others
are these blind and deaf. We will see and we will walk
because we will begin to understand that creation groans
until it reorients itself into the direction for which it was
ordained. Continual disorder and disorientation occasion a formlessness that renders a day, a month, and
the years meaningless. A recent novel about the Sioux
has the tribal wise man say to a young brave: Choose one
path and stay on it. In this you will find wisdom.

There is paradox here. If we don't change, we do not
grow. Yet if we move from situation to situation, from
commitment to commitment, from relationship to relationship, from place to place, we become merely vaga-
bonds, and the constant changing disorders any integrity
that is at our foundation. Hindu wisdom has a story about
the man who seeks the star, Alcor. The teacher points to
larger stars near it until the student's eyes become
accustomed to the night skies and can focus on this
particular star. In the same way, the process to single-
heartedness about the reign of God is a gradual maturation which happens in those followers of Jesus whose
single focus ultimately becomes the consuming passion
of their lives.

Somewhere within our geographic and emotional

peregrinations lies the possible unification of the changes that must take place in life with the steadiness of purpose and direction necessary for integrity. Perhaps the rhetoric of one's life being totally for the kingdom of God sounds strange to the Christian who accepts participation in Sunday worship, tithing, missionary aid, and certain moral codes as the totality of religious practice. Yet the paradigm of what it means to be a Christian has changed. Like it or not, admit it or not, the winds of change have touched us. Instead of ranting and raving, it behooves us to study exactly what is happening in order to discern the Spirit apart from our human vagary and banal deceits. Making a correct judgment depends entirely on our fundamental comprehension that Jesus' teaching about the reign of God was his central message. God must be all in all. His utter obedience and single-hearted direction to this interpretation of reality brought him to the cross. The Christian can do and be no less. We cannot absent ourselves from involvement in the coming of the kingdom. External cult empty of this foundational truth quickly loses significance and the Christian no longer knows why they do what they do ritually. Even religious professionals cannot presume they have accepted the divine mandate. A priest once admitted he had no particular trouble with celibacy and its relationships, but that single-heartedness was an overwhelming religious task and one that demanded a great deal more of persons than whether or not they married. He was exactly right. To be single-hearted about the coming of the kingdom is the hardest thing Christians will ever have to do. The emotional or religious debris which has cluttered the years must be cleared away from the single focus that all life is about the reign of God.

The blind must see and the deaf hear. That gospel sentence translated for today means peace, justice, and freedom in each person and in all relationships around the globe. It is a kind of madness, perhaps, to live one's life with this meaning structure over against those who disavow that holiness has any impact beyond vague theisms, flickering candles, and pious dronings. It is amazing to witness how the daily praxis of religious mandate is quickly replaced by clacking sticks, moving stones, or lighting lights. Humans love to whack sticks together in front of a shrine. For whatever peculiar reasons deep in our psyches, the gesture seems to afford some pleasant feeling of religious accomplishment. Yet ritual is empty unless it expresses a profound faith within the devotee that issues in a way of life which offers alternatives to violence, greed, and barbarism. It is the serious follower of Jesus who begins to see life as gradually focused into a single vision: all life is about the reign of God.

Now perhaps this is nice language, but we have buses to catch, Christmas tree ornaments to buy, children to feed and educate, and legal forms to fill out. The older ladies in the church can help the blind and the poor. This brand of sloughing off commitment to a religious life is precisely the kind of shortsightedness that makes the faith groups of the world seem insipid to outsiders. What kind of church is it that encourages occasional warm feelings of godliness but lacks any tie whatsoever to the complex and difficult messages of the founder? Does church merely indicate a sociological grouping within which we identify ourselves but which in fact makes no demand upon the way we talk or the paths we decide to take?

Then this strange character, the eunuch, appears on the scene accompanied by unicorns and rhinoceroses and shows us someone in whom the message of the reign of God has become the overarching connotation of each day. The eunuch buys ornaments and runs for buses, but in rare, reflective moments the eunuch knows the tiny thread of direction and the single significance for each day. Though on many occasions we are unable to locate even a shred of the filament, some mysterious faith shows the direction again.Who and what is this God who in Jesus has asked so much of my life? If only God would stay in a shrine and not demand for this mysterious Wisdom a place in the everyday. We can go home from shrines; we can never escape the Holy One who enters the most prosaic situations of work and home.

Gradually as the mystery of the eunuch is revealed in us, we find certain results of a single vision. We are somehow more quietly reflective, even prayerful. We recognize that we are no longer saying prayers, but rather that prayer has become the foundation of who we understand ourselves to be. At some profound center of the self, there is a reservoir of peace and unpeace which flows into our every act. Our lives are less unexamined yet we feel them as ever more ambivalent. Beneath the ambivalences, however, is a faith and a structuring vision that lends purpose to our steps. We seem somehow to have become warmer and more loving at the same time as we have become freer and more detached.

The counsel of the gospel to be a eunuch for the kingdom of God means all of this. Let those who are married, heed. Let those who have vowed celibacy for religious reasons, heed. Let those who have never married, heed. The journey to the self is the only place to begin the journey to God. There is an aspect of that self which is eunuch, and this facet of ourselves must be discovered.

CHAPTER SIX

Lions and Lambs

"The sign that you have this virtue [obedience]
is patience, and impatience is the sign that you
do not have it."

Catherine of Siena in *The Dialogue*

GOD'S will is that lions and lambs lie down together.
The peace symbolized by the camaraderie of these
natural enemies is a sign of the possibility and the
presence of God's reign. We acknowledge our doubts and
reservations about such an amicable projection. Our
times have brought us to the painful realization that sin
is radically a part of who we are. Lions and lambs war
inside each of us, let alone among neighbors and nations.
Literally, what on earth did Isaiah envision in his description of contentious animals coming together peaceably
with a little child leading them? Calf and lion cubs growing up together, leopards and kids, cows and bears—
clearly these feral contradictions cannot be anything
other than the flimsy dreams of a beleaguered prophet
who hoped that the future would not be so bad as the
present.

God's will is easily stated: It is that the kingdom come.
The reign of God—God as all in all—is what is willed.
There is nothing arcane about the concept. We misunder-
stand it when we ask of God's will whether we should buy
a Chevy or an Olds, whether we should get married or
stay single, or whether we should take this job or that. We
claim we would do God's will if we could know it clearly.
We blame God when we can't identify any direction and

choose self-structured limbos to bemoan our uncertainties. We facilely explain life's natural occurrences as God's will. Tragic deaths of children and loved ones, illnesses, and tidal waves all bear the name. Our griefs, angers, and frustrations are thus at least focused, a focus that sustains us since, with this ascription, we are able to shout out our pain against a presumably blameworthy and identifiable object. If we become wise in our travails, we acknowledge that God is never the puppeteer who pulls the strings of our misfortunes. We need a theological language other than that of the permissive will of God to speak about suffering. To say God permits suffering but does not cause it seems banal in the midst of a crushing malaise. Sometimes we piously use the phrase "God's will" to excuse ourselves from personal responsibility. "It's God's will I got this job." "It's God's will I was fired." "God has some plans for me which I will eventually find." All these wonderfully specious excuses take us off the dread hook of bearing responsibility for our words, choices, and behaviors in all the situations in which we find ourselves.

God's will is that lions and lambs lie down together; our task is to figure out how to facilitate the unity of the lion and lamb in ourselves and in all neighbors and nations. To define the will of God this way changes our entire worldview. No longer can we mumble that we want to do God's will if only we could know it. It is known, and we are to give our lives to it with the utmost honesty and commitment.

This conceptualization of the theological topic—the will of God—is yet another milestone in our journey to the self and into God. One's worldview must be oriented into this single vision of reality. Cling to our old notions as tenaciously as we might, our search for God's will has ended. The task is to get on with the things of the kingdom so that our religious practice issues in the flowering of peace and justice. Daily prayers and daily good deeds are authentic only as they are increasingly channeled into this purpose and direction.

Jesus became obedient to death—even a death by means of a cross. His obedience does not exemplify an inert body being propelled along a preordained path, so that one thinks of this death with its scandalous circumstances as eternally set in motion by Abba. Instead, Jesus lived a certain way each day; he taught and preached particular insights about God. His daily choices and actions to be for the reign of God set his religious opponents' teeth on edge, led to their charges of blasphemy and eventually to his murder at their hands. It takes a definite mindchange for us to view Jesus' mission this way. We have been content with our puppet notions; we like to think that God sent Jesus and that God knew we would do Jesus in, but that the whole affair would be ultimately salvific for us perpetrators of the crime. We witness the scenario, feeling sorry for Jesus while yet praising the redemption that graced us in this sacrificial action.

It is dreadfully shortsighted, though not necessarily incorrect, to view the history of Jesus as thus programed. The confident martyr portrait removes us from identification with him in an equally sacrificial and dedicated life, and thus from any personal conviction that the obedience of Jesus is incumbent upon us all.

Jesus' total being was consecrated to the reign of God. He came among us and is our very flesh so that lions and lambs might lie down together. God's reign was not set up because of his preordained death but because Jesus understood that for the kingdom to be present demanded of him and of his followers a definitive revelation of the nature of God. Jesus as Son knew God uniquely and supremely. He spoke of God as One who shattered all the categories of self-sufficient righteousness that the religious types had structured. Their preferments of themselves over sinners and any other riffraff of their society set them up for the condemnations uttered by Jesus. Jesus never withdrew his statements, amended them or apologized for them. He announced unequivocally the presence of God mediated in the poorest, the most weary, the oppressed, and the sinners. Only the poor and humble of heart could yield their notions of reality to these signs of the kingdom. These *anawim* were they who with faith-eyes saw life differently from all others. The followers of God had a particular way to live each day as opposed to a particular way to light lights or to wear pieces of cloths on their heads. Jesus continually preached that God must be all in all and that religion has to do with a consistent obediential posture concerning God's reign. This posture demands of godly persons that daily life be redirected into particular frames of reference and into very specific choices and actions. Such an obedience does not take us away from the geographical or relational situations in which we find ourselves; it does ordain, structure, and govern the attitudes with which we deal with every single person and event.

Jesus had a single direction in his mind and heart that shaped every word and act; we are summoned to the very same obedience. It is so much simpler to deal with God by parading ceremoniously in churchly corridors than to allow ourselves to be captivated completely by the vision of the lions and the lambs. It is so much easier to obey the jots and tittles than to ask the hard questions of life. The happening of the reign of God demands the commitment of our every waking moment so that we place no obstacle, nor do we thwart in any way the extension of God's reign. We are to confront head-on the lions and lambs inside ourselves and in all others and work at the peace-bearing liaison.

We hate religion thus to demand of us: "Just give some money to the poor. Send the children to Sunday school. Ring the bells. Sing the hymns. Forget the impossible demands of lions and lambs. No one can do this. We are not Jesus." As we too quickly note, the lions and lambs have not been cavorting happily together since Jesus' time. Was Jesus perhaps an idle dreamer, albeit the Son? Why must we live in the world with a different vision of reality from that of the pagans? To compound our complaints, the pagans have become increasingly difficult to pick out from the crowd. Apparently most of the crowd are pagans, even including many women and men who are presently carrying identification cards signifying memberships in churches. If Jesus could not establish the reign of God upon the earth, then who of us can? Just like the early followers, our expectation is for a kingdom that has no suffering and no pain, no disease or injustice.

One legitimately asks whether the circumstances of his death changed how Jesus understood the nature of God. Perhaps up until the end Jesus held some idea that Abba would reach out to save over against the natural occurrences of history as it winds along its inexorable way. But in his horrendous death Jesus perhaps recognized God forever submerged in the details of history just as it is. Yet this God, with grace and love, gives the possibility to find Abba available in abandonment, to find life in death and to know power in utter weakness. This theology causes us to change our minds about the meaning of following Jesus. The paradigm, member of church, has forever been changed by the obedience of Jesus. The disciples are to be Jesus. We are to live out in our own lives what Jesus lived out in his. He preached in word and taught in action about God who is accessible, available, and loving in all of the people and situations where our containments of the divine have not permitted its entrance. He taught a God present in the irrational as well as the rational of human history. He taught a God present in absence. He taught a God eloquent in dumbness and powerful in nothingness. What is the meaning of these paradoxes? Why can't God fit the accepted social molds of propriety and conformity? Why does God continually thwart our categories? Though we try to manipulate God into our image, God transcends our craft. Often God intervenes and acts in our personal and corporate histories in ways we would seldom choose.

This theology of the cross clarifies our task with the lions and the lambs. Jesus stood in the great tradition of his ancestors who envisioned an eventual reign of God. They sought this outcome of human events not purely in the interests of the divine but clinging as well to some hope for personal benefit. Jesus committed himself to God's reign to the end, perhaps beyond even his own ideas of its parameters. Having done this, he freed humankind forever from its shortsightedness and its limitations placed on the possibilities of God. He brought the rational and the irrational together in a proper and final articulation of the will of God. So irrational was what happened to Jesus that our containments of divine interventions were exploded beyond the boundaries of sense. "My God, my God, why have you abandoned me?" We call out this prayer when the irrational threatens our equilibrium. Destruction and death engulf us; the God who is God is right in it all. Why?

God's providence undergirds history encompassing both order and disorder. Through a kind of chiaroscuro of events we come to know ourselves. Each incident— joyous or tragic—affords us an opening to self-knowledge and the transcendent possibility of approaching the threshold of the divine, in the epitome of our own minds. This antechamber of the divine has been referred to as the *apex mentis* by spiritual writers through the centuries. We are forced to this heightened place of our own consciousnesses by the events and persons of our days. Within our developing interiority we are able to assess our days and our times with a deeper faith.

In this inner chamber we learn that our lives are not centered on ourselves and our changes toward personal maturation. The kingdom in our midst is interconnected with the happening of the kingdom in the heart of every global sister and brother. We have not been created to gratify our whims but to be Jesus, that is, to be son or daughter of God as Jesus is son. Our baptisms have given us this relationship to God. Our lives take on an urgency that the blind see, the deaf hear, the prisoners be freed, the lame walk, and the poor hear this good news. We become obedient the way Jesus was obedient. We know what life is about and we sense ourselves confirmed in the same vision that brought Jesus to the cross. The cross might also be for us the consequence of the way we choose to live our lives. There are subtle ways of our being crucified today; we may not be hung on the corner telephone pole but we may be delivered to the courts and churches of the powerful and the mighty. We are called fools and naive dupes of the communists as we take our stands against any political philosophy, whether capitalist or communist, that threatens the well-being and dignity of humankind. We may be crucified, mocked, and scourged as we work tirelessly for women's rights. We may be overlooked or ignored as we stand against the poisoning of our earth or against the destruction of humanity by the insanity of nuclear weaponry. "Left of center" becomes our label.

The positions we choose are embraced no matter the cost. Anguished searches after truth, vast reading and study, the common good as opposed to vested interest—all efforts bring us to the intellectual and emotional positions in which we find ourselves—dupes of nothing other than our own convictions, our own humanity, and our own painful search after God. We have mysteriously been brought to the place where lions and lambs gamboling together begin to make more sense than the deceits and pious lies of the war-mongering world powers.

Catherine of Siena again comes forward to offer her wisdom: "You will know you are obedient if you are patient." We recall Adrienne Rich's poem, "Integrity," with its wonderful opening line: "A wild patience has taken me thus far." Apparently for both these women, patience never connoted sitting back idly while the world passed them by. That Catherine succeeded in getting Pope Gregory XI to leave Avignon in order to move toward a single papacy demanded indeed a wild patience. From our historical perspective we see how wild a patience was necessary since, after Catherine's death, Robert of Geneva, a man feared and loathed throughout Italy for his murders of the innocent, returned to Avignon as Pope Clement VII. The lions and lambs she worked to unite went back to their separate popedoms. Does justice then never triumph over injustice? Does goodness never win? The expectations that everything will go our way are shattered by the multiple personalities and conflicts which force us to deal differently with the people and situations we face. Out of all the stress, we begin to recognize that the one who has changed is myself. The one who has matured, seen new visions and dreamed new dreams is I. Obedience, patience, self-knowledge, and the journey to God are all interrelated concepts.

Catherine had evidently prayed Hebrews 10:36: "You need patience to do God's will and to receive what God has promised." Obedience thus means to become one with God's will of establishing a kingdom of justice, peace, and freedom in every human heart and in every situation. We are obedient, that is, one with this providence if we are patient as we go about the task. Obviously, patience needs to be redefined. It has everything to do with getting up each morning and, even sluggishly, jumping into the breach of this obediential posture once again. Being strapped to the mast and getting our necks into the yokes are not metaphors we like to use, yet patience never desists from being for the kingdom. It never gives up, never swerves from its intention; it is steadfast. The patient woman or man becomes strangely self-possessed in the maddening, threatening, or nonsensical events of each day. Patience, like the undercurrent of a deep river, moves in a steady direction no matter the twists and turns. Catherine knew that if a person was not patient there would be no obedience, that is, no commitment to the reign of God. Impatient persons would hunger and thirst after justice for a while, but eventually their natural zests would wane, their course become unsteady and their determination fail.

The vulnerable spot for the obedient is the potential lack of patience. How long can someone committed to peace between lions and lambs remain faithful to the effort? The greatest threat to patience is the sense of feeling foolish about the enterprise anyway. The days are long, the task limitless, the companions vacillating, and the divine direction often garbled. Perhaps the world is banal and senseless. Take from it whatever pleasure and well-being is possible; maybe the hedonist choice is a proper and sensible course. But there remains patience—inexorable, steady, constant patience—a virtue containing something of the very life of God. Patience resists the gesture to throw in the towel. The inner spring moves on a sometimes fierce, sometimes gentle course—but it remains consistently active. It is tangible every day in taking out the garbage or in voting at the local precinct. Over many years, patience shapes words and daily practices into concerted purpose. Wisdom now combines with patience to form the truly obedient man or woman. Here is the person whose will is God's will, who has become one with God's designs, who patiently goes after the recalcitrant lions and lambs.

The connotation given obedience thus extends beyond churchly confines; however, the dialectic between lawfully constituted ecclesial authority and the obedience of the Christian gives a glimpse of the redemptive possibilities involved in the relationship. Church authority properly understood is gift given by the Spirit of God and by the community in order that the reign of God be proclaimed and the afflicted healed. As the tensiveness

between authority and obedience continues throughout
the history of the church, and such tensiveness is vital to
the life of the church, the drama of Jesus' becoming
obedient even unto death is re-presented in the life of
each Christian. No obsequiousness here which guarantees to authority figures the divine right of kings! The
thesis is that any ecclesial authority is for the extension
of the reign of God and that it has no other purpose or
place. Authority in an ecclesial context is not given to keep
the dullards in line, though historically the dialectic has
often been so employed. If the concepts are correctly
understood then indeed the relationships of authority
and obedience continue to have redemptive possibilities.

Many would disclaim: "Obey the rules. If you don't,
you'll be sorry. Never mind 'tensiveness between authority and obedience.' Do what the pope says. If you don't, at
least admit your sin and accept your guilt."

Over the centuries women and men have scored the
nights with their tears and questions about the rightness
of the dictates of authority and, as they sought their own
freedom before God, the struggle became the very avenue
for maturation and freedom if they were searingly honest
and open to the advent of the wisdom of God. Obviously
this thinking does not refer to the shiftless and the emotionally angry whose self-rejections structure their every
action. Nor does it point at popes, bishops, or pastors as
always errant while those in the pews are inculpable. The
significance of the word dialectic is just that: There is a
continual tensive relationship between authority and
obedience, the fruit of which is often a greater clarity in
knowing God's will.

A growing sadness is that so many of the community of
faith seem to possess no personal sense of following

Jesus. To them, the words in this chapter are meaningless —lions and lambs, obedience, authority, patience, self-knowledge, religious experience, or the will of God. These persons find no religious conflict in screaming racist epithets in the doorways of churches nor in disrupting eucharistic liturgies at which someone of different color is in attendance. The teachings of Jesus, the magisterium of the church, and what nitty-gritty life is all about are totally out of focus for many nominal Christians. The onlooker is drawn to the cynicism of the Grand Inquisitor and to the desire to give the faithful just what they want: magic, miracles, and authority. The story reveals the connotation of authority as indeed that which dullards have over them and against which they sin in a kind of engaging, devotional game-playing. One comprehends why religion and religious practice thus ill-defined so often bring serious people to agnosticism or atheism.

We must be in touch with our own personal religious experience in order to know the self-journey at all; otherwise, religion is always something outside of us. We are dependent on authority figures to tell us about God and the things of God. We have little or no personal religious sense gained from our own struggles with life and our faith assessment of these. We need a deeply convicted sense that God has acted in our lives and has led us along particular paths to enlightenment, purification, and a graced existence. Though we may perceive the meaning of our days only in hindsight, nonetheless we know our experiences to be authentic, and we know indeed that divinity has been mediated to us through the multiple instances and persons who have happened in our lives.

We are aware that the world is full of peculiar individuals who name their own oddities and emotional peculiarities, divine interventions. It is at this juncture that the scrutiny of the church community through the centuries has proved invaluable in testing the truth of spiritual assertions. Yet we also know that many people with authentic visions have been persecuted. Many of the mystics and contemplatives of our tradition, though truly imbued with God's power, were condemned or sorely tried through many years for the visions of reality that were in their hearts, placed there indeed by the wisdom and providence of God. Sometimes only after their deaths was the community able to accept their word as authentic and to admit that in this human being God had once again visited the people.

It takes strongly convicted women or men to hold to their insights which have been verified by their own religious experience over against the dictates of the church community. These persons are either very integrated or very mad, and conflicts between personal religious experience and authority have occurred many times in ecclesiastical history. I am referring to all incidents—from reports that St. Peter appeared in the front hall closet to struggles for purity of conscience in all decisions. We can only watch and wait for time to bear out the truth of our visions. Many church persons, I'm sure, thought Catherine nothing other than pushy and way out of line when she took on the popes of the 14th century. What right had she, a woman, to tell popes what to do? Yet here was Catherine called to obedience and blessed with patience standing against the papal schism. In addition, she called the clergy to task in her *Dialogue* with such vehemence that even today the clergy would find her diatribe embarrassing.

The point is that one's obedience is in direct proportion to one's personal religious experience. Only as we recognize the God-directed dimensions of our lives, sense them, welcome them, and name them are we able to interpret the significance of ecclesiastical dictate and recognize when ecclesiastical rigor is nothing other than sin out of which only error has come to the church or when ecclesiastical dictate is in fact for the life and growth of the People of God.

Who or what is to be the measure of our decisions? There isn't any clear path. One does not go against the teachings of the hierarchy cavalierly. In the recent past, for example, the magisterium has spoken of the rights of women and men to unionize, of the error of controlling births by other than natural means, of the destructive madness of nuclear weaponry. Where does the Catholic stand in relationship to any and all of these statements?

In the last analysis, it is God's will that we must seek. God's will is that the blind see, the deaf hear, the lame walk, and the poor hear the gospel of love and salvation. Obedience is completed in us on the day when that will has become our will. Obviously the ramifications of such obedience are endless but the follower of Jesus knows her/himself to be on a sure path. All rules and regulations fall into place now. At least the lions and lambs inside oneself are able to nod at each other on some occasions. It is only from this peaceable inner meeting that other lions and lambs might take example. Here is a person whose life testifies to the authenticity of the journey to self. God is here. We've seen a lion and lamb or two lying down together.

CHAPTER SEVEN

Doves and Ravens

"The Holy Spirit which Abba will send in my
name . . . will remind you of all that I told you."
Jesus, in John 14

JESUS knew well our need to be reminded of all he told
us. Like the pagans, we followers of Jesus desire a kingdom of this world, one that satisfies our cravings for
everyone and every event going our way here and now.
The alternative is not a kingdom beyond the grave as we
have most often interpreted the "not of this world." The
reign of God is to be found in history with a faith that does
not compel historical detail to correspond with our wills
but with eyes that perceive in each day, whatever its detail,
the impress of the divine.

We must be reminded of this reality—about 365 times
annually—that there is an aspect of the mystery of God
immanently present to our evolving personal and
corporate histories. We have named this presence of
Holy Mystery immanent within our lives, the Holy
Spirit. Once the name is spoken, however, we pull out
our tried-and-true religious notions in order to fashion
this aspect of God with our definitions and confine-
ments. This limiting accomplished, we are content that
mystery is once again under control. We are uncomfort-
able with truth that eludes management.

Through the centuries some art has portrayed the
Triune God as three male persons, one older and venerable, obviously the Father and Creator; one young and
bearded, Jesus; and one middle-aged gentleman whom

96

uneasily we referred to as the Holy Ghost. Since it has been difficult, if not downright peculiar, to allude to a male personification as "Ghost" or "Spirit," we, employing the scriptural symbols, graphically illustrated this third aspect of God as a tongue of fire or a dove. This led one little girl to remark: "I understand about the Father and the Son, but I don't even think the Spirit eats with them." An understandble quandary! A Japanese gentleman was heard to say:"Honorable Father, I understand. Honorable Son, I understand. Honorable Bird, I do not understand at all."

These anecdotes emphasize our confusions in speaking of the Spirit, the One sent to remind us of the imperative of the reign of God and of Jesus' proclamation of it. Moreover, a good amount of trinitarian preaching has subjected us to a dreadful "Tom, Dick, and Harry" rhetoric which we abhor but into which we find ourselves tangled before we can hear our own inculpable yet heretical tritheism. We know we're in trouble when we listen to how well "they" get along and what love and community "they" have among "them" and "why can't we improve our communication with one another modeled on the life of the Trinity?" Yet we struggle for a proper language because faith in the mystery of Trinity is deep and sure, however inarticulate. We are hampered by the sparseness of our language of Three Persons in One God and by the connotation given person in our language which confine us to a minimal faith-understanding.

The centuries-old definition of the doctrine of Trinity was hard won, indeed. The least educated among us has heard something of the painful struggles, sin, and deceit as the community of Jesus in the first few hundred years worked to safeguard their faith by structuring into it the buttresses of theological, philosophical, historical, and linguistic disciplines. Though some may denigrate these efforts, we must admit in our better moments that, more often than not, the church has been saved from a careless fundamentalism because of its vast theoretical explanation of itself. Naturally the explanations can become overbearing and pretentious; some persons have even presumed them to be all-encompassing of life's questions. For the most part, however, theologians have done the community of faith a great service through many centuries. The tensions between simple faith and the theological effort have led to a proper and sure course through the shoals of human vagaries.

The thinkers in the early church, witnessing the actions of God in creation, redemption, and sanctification and based upon the words of Jesus, told us that in God there were three *hypostaseis*, a word we have rendered, person. Each of us blithely confesses to three persons in one God—not of course Tom, Dick, and Harry, but most of the time sounding dangerously close to this aberration of the truth. Upon discovering ourselves hovering on the brink of tritheism we back away, vaguely mumbling something about three-leaf clovers, three rivers running into one ocean or three of anything that will hold to unity while confessing trinity. Ultimately we nicely relegate the whole question to mystery and declare a moratorium on trying to come any closer to the sacred.

It might be a felicitous occurrence if the Greek, *hypostasis*, could remain untranslated. When we would speak of three *hypostaseis* in God, we would have no mental image at all of what the word connotes. This might spare us the problematic images of the older and middle-aged male persons or the older male person and a dove or a tongue of fire for the Ghost. Obviously we have not successfully penetrated the meaning of "person" when it refers to the divine. Our understanding is aided by Vedantin Hindus who refer to Brahman as "impersonal," yet who do not mean by this definition to imply an amorphous or amoeba-like presence in the sky. The word, impersonal, denotes that the Absolute has no relationship with humankind. Thus, to speak of a personal deity is to declare that the divine is related to us. From the revelation of our Jewish forebears and extended to us in Jesus' teaching comes the faith that our God is indeed related to us and this, in terms of loving kindness and fidelity.

"Person" then should connote relationship to us rather than Tom's, Dick's, or Harry's. Try as we will to envision nicer, kinder, more loving persons than our aunts and uncles and analogically to reach for a God-concept, God escapes even our analogies and that is a happy fact. We are too prone to manipulate the divine, yet God has always been before and beyond each one of our attempts to whittle the deity to our own size and specifications.

Karl Rahner tells us that the Trinity of the economy of salvation is the immanent Trinity. God is what God does. We have spied out three actions of divinity—creation, redemption, and making whole and holy. All three are aspects of the economy of our salvation. We have said that the one God has three countenances. One of these we have called Abba, because Jesus called it Abba. This countenance tells us that Holy Mystery is available. The terms Mother, Father, or Abba are terms that signify relationship and availability. Thus we state our credence unequivocally that this *hypostasis* of the divine is related to us benevolently, that is, is available to us with loving kindness. To call God Abba is to signify primarily relationship and availability, not maleness.

The second countenance of the divine we know by the

name Jesus, which means "Yahweh saves." This aspect of Holy Mystery has become one of us, a mystery of eternal kindness that escapes our wildest hopes and dreams. We so facilely speak of God's becoming a man; our tongues have announced it so frequently in song and prayer that the credal statement has become commonplace. If we think about it, the assertion is beyond our grasp; it renders us breathless and overwhelmed in reverence, awe, and adoration. With a totally gracious providence, Holy Mystery has so embraced humankind as to become one with it forever. Other religious dispensations boast of gods coming to earth, but none that became and remained human while retaining divinity, and both of these forever. Whatever incarnation is all about, it compels us to silence and a prostration of heart and mind. One of the *hypostaseis* of the divine is what I am!

The third countenance of Holy Mystery is radically and immanently present to the unfolding of our personal and corporate history. We have named this *hypostasis* in God, Holy Spirit. Our personal history takes place in time; each day we move into relationships, oppositions, tensions, and connections between self and other events and persons. Each of these instances is a developmental possibility. We act, interact, and are acted upon; the happenings constitute our personal histories. As persons and events are integrated into the becoming that is our processive identity, an *hypostasis* in God is radically present to the integration. Faith names the Holy Spirit as that eternal Integration in which the integration of our lives occurs. Our disintegrations are factors in the integrity and in our becoming whole and holy. This work of sanctification has traditionally been defined as that of the third *hypostasis* in God. The totality of our lives, wonderful or sorrowing, is the content of our integration and of our holiness.

Religious people are at a crisis period. Either their faith statements inform each day with significant choices and actions, or churchly involvement and the tenets of religion become simple pleasantries offering thin comfort to those who put a dollar in the collection plate. As Christians of our times, we refuse to banish the entire dispensation of faith to a comfortable palaver deprived of any effective praxis. Further, we will not allow the magnificent body of knowledge which theology (faith seeking understanding) has developed through centuries to be merely an antiquated rhetoric irrelevant to these times. The great *Summae*, catechisms, treatises, histories, and biographies must be transmitted so that the past lends its wisdom to the questions of the present and to the structures of the future. Either the entirety of the deposit of faith has everything to do with daily life or religion over the centuries has indeed been the opiate of the people.

Persons of faith view history as bearing the impress of the divine. Bonaventure saw in the earth the *vestigia Dei*, the evidences of the divine, and humanity was more than mere evidence. Women and men were the *imago Dei*, the icon of God. "Whoever has seen me, Philip, has seen Abba." The words of Jesus can be said by us. We are daughters and sons by reason of baptism.

John's gospel says that no one can understand about the reign of God unless that person is born from on high. The passage is an acknowledgement of that gracious power which has raised us beyond the temporal in order to be able to view all reality in the context of the reign of God. Our capability for this specific worldview is the result of the Spirit's work of making whole and holy. God is what God does. The Spirit is what the Spirit does. The Holy Spirit, the third *hypostasis* in God is immanent, that is, right within the warp and the woof of our personal history. Anything less than this overwhelming insight reduces this aspect of the divine to some occasional intervention but certainly denies to Holy Mystery any immediate relevance to the continuous dialectic of persons and events over against one's individualized consciousness.

God is as near as the next knock at the door, the first plaguing person or event of the day, the joyous surprise that gives laughter, the attempts to understand and to make self understood by the other, or the fear of our human diminishment. Our histories force us to deal with the tensiveness between our individual consciousness and that of others as well as with the dialectic between ourselves and all events. What happens as a result of the multiple interactions daily, monthly, and annually is that, in dealing with the plethora of happenings, we come to know ourselves. This last phrase may seem so insignificant. We want it to read: "We come to know others," or "We come to know God," or "We become wiser," or "We give ourselves over to the works of justice and peace." In fact, all these eventualities are intertwined. Their occurrence is simultaneous, though all are dependent on self-knowledge; without this basic and primary journey, our other ventures are grounded in illusion.

Faith informs life. We see life differently because we are persons of faith. There is no more accurate insight into the meaning of the journey to the self and into God than that provided by a proper pneumatology. The identification of God as immanent to our becoming, and this, in the most normal and prosaic events of each day, allows us to welcome our becoming whole and holy as God's intention and love. We do not like this intention and love in the disintegrating times; with Lucy in the Peanuts cartoon, we prefer only ups and no downs. In the process of becoming whole and holy, we are readied for the act of justice in the world. This does not imply our waiting to get life together before becoming involved in our world. Rather, the self-journey becomes the avenue to that self-denial or self-transcendence that contains the possibility for justice. When we recognize the immanent God in the self-journey, only then are we rooted in that personal integrity necessary to the act of justice. In biblical terms, only then are we born from on high and able to acknowledge the reign of God in its earthly epiphanies.

Noah sent out a raven to test for land beyond the flood. It flew around and around. There was no solid place to land. He then sent a dove which returned to the Ark. How alight on a moving stream? How rest in a rushing flood? Finally, the dove came back with an olive branch in its beak. Ravens and doves and we women and men need a sure base from which to make our life journey. The sure base is self-knowledge. Without it we erect castles in the air and phantom kingdoms in the mind, but the proclamation of the reign of God is far from us. We hide from the dialectic between self and other. We put up barriers named shyness, celibacy, marriage, distrust, sexual identity, piety, or church laws against relating to people and events that would cause us to change and grow. We think that if we batten down the hatches of our arks and never send out any ravens or doves that we will be safe in our individuality. The result of our precautions is, of course, stultification and a choice for death rather than life. Our ark floats on an ambivalent sea which we fear to question.

Another dove, however, enters the picture: "I saw the spirit descend like a dove from the sky, and it came to rest on Jesus." There is a connection between the "rest" which Noah's dove sought and the dove which "rested" on Jesus. In this connection we find a hint about where humanity ultimately finds its meaning.

With this symbol of a dove, John describes the power from on high that touched the humanity of Jesus giving it its messianic summons to the proclamation of the reign of God and to the healing of the afflicted. In the death of Jesus God reveals the nature of immanence. In the cross Abba suffers the pain of the death of Jesus and the third *hypostasis* in God, eternally the Love between Abba and Jesus, proceeds in the gathering of all human history, personal and corporate, into the mystery of the Godhead. God is not far off and unattainable. One *hypostasis* in God, because of the death of Jesus, is forever within the context of human existence perceived with the eyes of faith.

These words are hard. It is perhaps the better part of wisdom to consign the meaning of trinity to mystery interpreted as impregnable and forever concealed. But if our God-language has nothing whatever to do with us then we ought to wrap up the theological effort once and for all. We should deny to faith any understanding and be content with a religious life that has absolutely nothing to do with ordinary life but which serves as a sort of social gratification for our devotional needs one morning or evening a week. We recall, again, however, Rahner's insistence that "the Trinity of the economy of salvation is the immanent Trinity."

At Jesus' baptism the dove, searching for the person who will undertake the messianic effort for the kingdom of God, came to rest upon Jesus thus designating him as the Way for all believers to discover the meaning of their own journey. Scholastic theology has spoken of Jesus as the exemplary cause of our salvation. The way Jesus lived, preached, died, and rose becomes not merely the model for how we ought to go about things; Jesus is the empowerment which causes us to be involved in the salvific enterprise in each succeeding era. The community of disciples tries to remain faithful to, and continually be reminded of, all that Jesus told us and revealed to us.

The Spirit rests or resides within our daily lives. The Spirit reminds us of the meaning of Jesus and of the nature of our lives as followers. This is all very ordinary— no whispered messages nor fluttering wings. Hopkins, in his powerful poem, "Peace," speaks of the Spirit coming with work to do. The work is that of enlightening the mind to see God's reign and enlivening the heart in order that we can be given over to the things of God—all of this while fishing, getting the oil changed, celebrating birthdays, and boycotting products whose manufacturers care little for human health and dignity. Thomas Merton praised this Spirit in a song he named, "A Whitsun Canticle." The Spirit is all the presence and power that changes our dust and nothing into fields and fruit. Changing a tire is not what it seems!

The proximity of God to our days seems sometimes too much to think about. It is a truth of overwhelming beauty yet a truth that is elusive enough to get lost in the daily details unless faith is summoned to ferret out presence even in what looks to be absence.

Certainly, the language of indwelling is lyrically preferable to that of *hypostasis*. The Spirit indwells our lives. This indwelling is not to be imaged as a bird in a cage. Indwelling signifies that the third *hypostasis* in God, one of the countenances of the divine, is immanent within our personal history. We like to recognize this indwelling on those days when all is going smoothly, when no one is making demands, and when contradiction and conflict seem far off. But our days contain pressures, tedium, fears, controversies, minutiae, and determinations to be made; whatever indwelling is all about, we certainly don't feel it at these times. God is, however, immanent to our lives. It is useful to examine some of the places where we ordinarily would not identify presence, power, and life.

One such place would be those moments when ultimate questions assemble on the parameters of our existence and we begin to see them just out of the corner of our eye. As these questions threaten us, fear tugs at our heartstrings.

"Who am I and where am I going?"

"What is life all about?"

"I am going to die; I have fewer years ahead of me than behind me."

"My life is changing. My loved ones are going their separate ways. Some of them will die before me."

"Is there God?"

"Are faith and church hoaxes?"

"Is the reign of God indeed occurring? Has it ever occurred? Has it been merely a hope and a dream from deep within humanity that things could be different from the way they are?"

These fears can be called crises of faith or mid-life crises, if desired. The experiences of our human diminishment and all that is concomitant with it bring us to the brink of despair. Faith must now be summoned to assert that Holy Mystery is indeed radically present within each stage of our becoming, including even our diminishment. Small comfort, perhaps, but oddly confirming. Underlying our fear is a confirmation of presence which though it does not halt our diminishment, confirms the meaning of it. A new stage of integration through disintegration has been achieved. Face lifts, false eyelashes, or corsets to hold in a paunch reveal their pathetic humor. Nothing external gives meaning. Only the journey to self, the process of integration and interiority and self-knowledge which can lead to self-transcendence allow us to be ready for the self-gift which aging and death demand of us. None of the journey has been meaningless. God accompanied the way within every detail and circumstance. We may feel futile, but immanence guarantees that God is present in futility, offering the potential to draw significance even from the absurd. We grow; we change. We become woman or man. Integrity happens oftentimes without our recognition. We call out: "Who can believe this?" Yet this is the faith of the Christian. Far more than credal lists, the faith demanded affirms meaning over meaninglessness. Faith is not sight or insight; it is not understanding though it continually seeks understanding. Faith is simply what it implies—the leap in the dark to the assertion of meaning. "I believe, Lord; help my unbelief" is all we can whisper. It is enough. Holy Mystery is not absent.

We forget indwelling when disorder and disruption engulf our days. We like a God who goes along with our plans. We resent the God of disruption and disorder. Housekeeping disorders or whether the drapes are hanging in a straight line is not the point. The disorders are within—emptiness, depression, vague unnameable blues, and the disjunctions that threaten the controls we've exerted externally. In addition, there are disorders and disruptions in our global community that threaten the future of humankind. Because of the collective unconscious of humankind, or what Christians have called the communion of saints or the mystical body of Christ, we know humanity to be interconnected. What happens to a global sister or brother has universal effect. Each of us is disordered and disrupted in the disorder and disruption of the globe.

If we experienced perhaps two disruptions yearly, we might be able to cope, but when disorder and disruption within and outside plague us with unlimited frequency, our stability as person is threatened. Yet from deep within a personal creative maturity arises in which we find some ability to give order to disorder and form to what is formless. God is radically present in this ability. Our personal creative maturity occurs in the Spirit who breathed form into chaos in original creation. As order is created in our personal history, we recognize the presence of the One we have called the third Person in the Blessed Trinity.

We do not presume that doves bearing olive branches of change and peace are flying all about like pigeons in a park. However, there are perceptible changes both personally and societally that faith acknowledges. When persons from all walks of life, all colors, all creeds, all classes join against nuclear weaponry and for peace, or when as individuals we see ourselves brought beyond the disorders and disruptions that threaten personal stability and this, by very small olive branches that turn up oddly in the doorways of our minds—all these are instances of the Holy Spirit undergirding and indwelling human existence in very daily and ordinary ways.

We recall the word *grace* from our religious vocabulary. We like grace to be contained within the dimensions of acceptability. However, grace often comes as interruptor, as annoyance, as change, as irrational or as that which reverses. Such graces as well as the easier graces enable the self-journey unless we resist and refuse this interruptive grace entrance. Grace is kept at bay by ruses of guilt, rejection, or games we play. As example—a priest imagines he spends his life lusting, which then allows him to wallow in guilt. Pathetically enough, no one is lusting after him, but useless guilt fends off change or growth. After all, if we didn't spend psychic energy every day being guilty, what would we do with our time? In the scenario, guilt becomes an armor against new directions and greater maturity. There is so much more to life, but this person has chosen guilt as the prism through which to view reality. No self-journey here. Sometime long ago a choice was made to hide behind the guilt, bless it, and indulge in self-pity to the end because of the pain of life choices. A trivial path indeed. Obviously, the example is not reserved to clerics. Kept at bay because of human decision, the Spirit broods over such an existence.

Grace is thwarted by the shells of righteousness and

comfortability that religious folks build around themselves. We give to charity, we make retreats; we are the
good people of society compared to the sinners and the
riffraff. We cling tenaciously to our bailiwicks of self-
sufficiency lest our respectability is threatened.

Both guilt and self-sufficiency are obstacles to self-
knowledge. Guilt and comfortability are, however, merely
the tips of icebergs, the depths of which lie in low self-
esteem, the violence of self-hatred, rigid controls placed
on self and life, and paralysis at the thought of being
known even by oneself. Grace can find its way through
the cracks in these shells if we allow it and are not terrified of its advent. When such grace enters, we identify the
occurrence—through the neighbors, or some children, or
a book in the mail or a cactus plant—as the immanent
presence of the divine in life cracking open in uncanny
and unpredictable ways the barriers we've erected.

A time when the acknowledgement of divine presence
is nearly impossible is in life's utterly incomprehensible
moments. Events occur that reduce explanation to
absurdity and cause literally unutterable pain. Note that
the words to describe these times are the same as we have
used to describe the transcendent God. God is inaccessible. God is unutterable. God is ineffable. These
sentences used in prayer have exploded God beyond our
ken and we have named this incomprehensibility,
transcendence. In human pain there is something of a
reverse transcendence as an insightful Carmelite nun
suggested. Indeed God is incomprehensible and unutterable, but these words now do not denote an intangible
place beyond grasp but rather the intangible and the in-
communicable that is a part of every day. Within life's
incomprehensibilities is the God who is incompre-

hensible. In moments when no word of explanation is utterable, God is indeed unutterable. We so hate to name these moments of extraordinary pain godly. Moreover, to do so does not alter the pain or bring explanation or surcease. However, we continue to walk on and, as no-explanation becomes integrated into the self-journey, we know an aspect of Holy Mystery immanent without our ability merely to continue.

Plato, in the mouth of Socrates, told us that an un-examined life is not worth living. Offered here is a particular examination of life. It is that of a Christian who believes that doctrines were meant to have relevance for daily life. Faith invests life with meaning, theology seeks to understand faith, and theology is constructed by the interpretations and theoretical explanations of the faith that is in the hearts of women and men in all eras and places and ways of life.

We need to identify Holy Mystery resident in our lives on those occasions when concrete acts of love are offered to us. We offer love to others, but when we become the recipient of love we often don't know what to do and find ourselves backing away. Love threatens all our dribs and drabs of self-hatred. The games we've learned to play to fend off another's gesture toward us go into operation. It is inconceivable that people outside our immediate family, neighborhood, or community should love us. We're often surprised that someone within those confines cares what happens to us. Our self-protection against intimacy comes to the fore: What if they should find us foolish? or stupid? or unlovely? or old? or too young? or weak? or daft? We also remember a time when we trusted an act of love and the experience blew up in our faces. We lost or had to let go of what we thought we loved. To love and to allow oneself to be loved is the hardest thing a human being has to do. But every success at it and every failure at it facilitates the self-journey. Through multiple encounters with small and large gestures of love offered and given, we come to know ourselves and we come to the possibility of transcending ourselves in genuine acts of love which we can offer, acts no longer rooted so deeply in our needs and cravings for approval and affirmation. The act of love given and received is a part of what God is.

All this seems unattainable to us. We are poor at this gesture of love which seems so simple. It's easier to conquer the world riding a herd of elephants than it is to become love. Love is what God is. The one who abides in love, abides in God. All of who we are, our sexuality, our emotional needs, our psychic wounds, our cast-iron preliminary antipathies, our empiricism—all must give way before this last great advent of the divine overtaking of the totality of our existence. We can become what God is. We can become love; the small and large forays into acts of loving are the pieces and parts of the self-journey. Some very old and wise people know this wisdom. It is a deeply experiential knowledge not easily come by, but every move toward it and every strength enabling us is evidence of Holy Mystery present within our feeble efforts and oftentimes preposterous ploys and blindnesses.

Can becoming what God is—becoming love—ever really happen to us? The mystics say, yes, and they were quite ordinary people. Catherine of Genoa came through deep personal neurosis and a dreadful marriage to a new place of wholeness and healing. So can we. This wholeness and healing is companion to the self-journey. It is the salvific work of the Spirit every day of our lives. There is an aspect, a countenance, an *hypostasis*, a Person in God we have called the Holy Spirit, that is radically a part of our becoming whole and holy as we journey to the center of the self and find there the threshold to Holy Mystery, available, one like ourselves, and immanent in our personal and corporate history. We have always called these three countenances of Holy Mystery, the Three Persons in One God.

CHAPTER EIGHT

Sparrows and Vultures

> The six wings of the Seraph can rightly be taken
> to symbolize the six levels of illumination by
> which, as if by steps or stages, the soul can pass
> over to peace through ecstatic elevations of
> Christian wisdom. There is no other path but
> through the burning love of the Crucified.
>
> Bonaventure in *The Soul's Journey into God*

IN the prologue to *The Soul's Journey into God*, Bonaventure speaks of that peace to which the scriptures point
and to which his mentor Francis continually adverted.
Bonaventure sought this virtue with those elevations of
Christian wisdom that had learned that peace is not a
pleasant feeling enrapturing the beginning of the self-
journey but rather that which would come "through the
burning love of the Crucified." We misread the phrase
when we cherish the cross of Jesus Christ historically but
miss the message that it is we who must choose to die, that
is, give our lives over to God and the reign of God no
matter the cost or our geographical situation. As the
lions and lambs revealed, any other peace but that found
in the cross, with the specific ramifications the word involves, is a poor and specious peace.

When we equate peace with fairyland dreams of plenty
and prosperity, whether internal or external, peace eludes
us. Bonaventure's description of the God who awaits us at
the end of the journey as a God of unknowing, of darkness, of silence and obscurity gives us the clue that the

peace experienced on the self-journey and on the journey into God is not a continual state of lightsomeness but one typified by words which suggest obscuration. Similar to Teresa's seventh mansion, the end of the journey brings us to deeper faith not to brighter visions. We don't like to hear this. As we approach nearer maturation we want to claim wonderful vistas of understanding. Peace, however, lies at the summit of faith.

Bonaventure's friend Thomas Aquinas, quoting Augustine, explained peace as the tranquillity of order. With his inimitable precision, Thomas distinguishes concord from peace. Concord exists among human beings when they can consent to the same things. Peace goes beyond this; it exists as the inner integrity or unity within each individual. All the facets of the human personality are ordered. Thomas would want us to know that a perfect inner order is not possible this side of eternity. However, the closer we approach God and the things of God, the more we experience this integrity, but we approach just as we are and in the obscurity of faith.

We may never interpret "coming closer to God" to mean that if we only worked harder at it or went to church more, we would be more godly. The language expresses the fact that peace is ours as we face honestly the self we are and know that, in its ups and downs, it is in God. It is we who parcel out what we will accept as godly and what we will discard and reject as ungodly. Surely there is much in us that is ungodly, but we come to peace only when we admit that everything about us is the material out of which a singular Providence fashions maturation. Peace does not cohabit with the violence of self-hatred nor with a pitiably low self-esteem. Bonaventure, Thomas, and

Teresa knew this well, but we place them on inaccessible pedestals and deny their ability to companion us through hard and complex days.

That the journey to the self and into God climaxes in peace and that there are many tangible evidences of this peace all along the way is certain, but the journey-person has abandoned the idea that peace is the opposite of troubled times. Peace is the proper integration of the multiple factors of human existence and thus "ordered." No one lives in unadulterated bliss. Peace is present where wisdom achieves an integration of the good and the difficult, of sunshine and storms, and of the multiplicity of temperaments and opinions into the whole that is named daily existence. We often feel life is an endless cycle of ups and downs, in which circularity our preference is obvious. Given our normal bias for the ups, we tend to locate peace only in comfortable times. Down moments, whether internal or in society, cause our thin feelings of repose to evaporate.

To be always unruffled or to cherish placidity is not at all what our spiritual forebears had in mind. Peace is hard-won. The journey to the self is an arduous and long one. Why do we so minimize peace as to equate it with unperturbed calm? True peace comes in direct proportion to self-knowledge; anything else may be brief surcease, but it is not peace.

Peace on a worldwide scale, however more complex, is nothing other than the totality of its integrated parts. We see at once the historical impossibility of this achievement. A ceasefire is poor peace indeed. Can there really never be world peace? In his poem, "Peace," Gerard Manley Hopkins names as adjunct to peace, patience. The poet pleads that the Lord should leave in lieu of peace some good: "And so God does leave patience exquisite, that plumes to peace thereafter." As Catherine of Siena knew the imperative of patience to obedience, as Adrienne Rich writes of a "wild patience," and as Dorothee Sölle names her splendid book of poems, *Revolutionary Patience*, so must we comprehend, however reluctantly, that patience is antecedent to, and constitutive of, peace. The work of peace, that is, the work of integrating all life's pieces and parts whether on a personal or worldwide scale is painstaking and time-consuming. Patience is indispensable.

Aquinas tells us how sorrow hinders our reason. We well know being bogged down by various levels of sorrowing and how, in those depressed times, reason is unable to come to our aid. It is here that Thomas places patience; it is the virtue that safeguards our reason in those fearful moments when we cannot find our way through the tangled briars of pain. Patience comes to our aid. Reason is enabled to admit the pain yet move in, through, and past it. As coordinate to peace, patience may not be stereotyped as a bright-eyed, pleasant do-nothing who by some stroke of fortune has sufficient resources to live insulated from humanity's pain-filled struggles. It is a dreadful error that interprets the power-filled human excellence which is patience as a hiding place for the indolent, the cowardly, or the dull of wit.

Perhaps the language of the beatitude that peacemakers shall be called children of God reinforces our misconception that peace and patience are quiet and unassuming virtues of natively gentle, little people. Hopefully, the enormity of our societal malaise can pry us away from our pacific impressions and bring us to understand that the peacemakers among us will be the most courageous and valiant women and men we know. Hotheads need not apply to work for peace; the peacemaker is one who is consistent, unswerving, and endlessly determined. The personality readied for this beatitude is to be found in the rare individual. This is not to excuse us all from the task, but to point up how difficult and extensive is the work of peace in our times.

Those who are adept through practice and by the grace of God at integrating the details of each day within themselves are persons of peace. These are they who have come to a compassion and a solidarity with others born of the ability to take the healthy and the unhealthy phases of life and bring them together at their personal centers. These are they who understand that the work of integration lies, not in forcing the absurd of human existence to make sense, but in fronting the absurd by allowing absorption and integration, change and growth within themselves. Others will deny the absurd of history, rail against it, demand that the absurd become rational and ultimately close eye, heart, and mind against it and choose a grumbling yet unproductive stagnation. Over against violence, torture, arms escalation, and greed, the peacemaker stands committed to a way of living that is utterly different. A fool? Perhaps, by some judgments. Fully human? This designation is closer to the truth.

My book, *I Am What I Do*, outlines a theology of the apostolic spirituality called contemplation. The text describes the integrative possibility to which some are brought by the grace of God become one with their own decisions and choices. These are the children of God, the sons and daughters of God who can bear the name peacemaker. The shallowness of the substitution "peacekeeper" for "peacemaker" is recognized for its inadequacy. To be a maker of peace demands a totally integrated spiritual journey that issues in the daily practice of those religious tenets which others fix in the reliquary of explicit but ineffectual orthodoxy. Peacemaking demands choices for actions which result in changes and conversions in the maker of peace.

The spirituality of peacemaking is identifiable by several components. One of these is that the peacemaker prays for peace but understands that prayer is a comprehensive way of living; thus, we cannot pray with our backs to the accumulated hopelessness of our world. Johannes Metz says his citizenry cannot pray with its back to Auschwitz. American citizens cannot pray with their backs to Nagasaki and Hiroshima. World citizens cannot pray with their backs to the threat of nuclear destruction. These statements signify that peacemaking is a highly complex business which lies well beyond a rosary to our Lady of Fatima or the recitation of St. Francis' Prayer for Peace. Both are excellent prayers. We must pray for peace, yet prayer does not in itself comprise the task of peacemaking.

The spirituality for the peacemaker demands change in our way of going about practically everything. We cannot stand apart from the world mumbling about the complexity of the issues and bemoaning our powerlessness. This infantile posture denies grandeur, hope, renunciation, effort, and all the dreams of the human spirit. A pious despair as response to the force of the military-industrial complex withholds from providential design any possibility for a new order. On the other hand, if we know history even casually we can admit without any great amount of insight that evil has triumphed over good again and again in the pages of our chronicles. This fact has sometimes led believers to wait for a "kingdom not of this world," that is, one beyond the grave. The followers of Jesus, however, know that the eschatological kingdom is "not of this world" because it lies yet ahead but in historical time. Its happening in the possible future is God's doing but participation in its occurrence is incumbent upon the disciple.

Thus, though peacemakers may score the night with impotent and frustrated tears, the task summons. Davids against Goliaths indeed! Goliath wins often, but it is by faith and not by numbers of victories that the peacemaker lives. When it comes to peacemaking, this believer is not deceived by the few bones political Goliaths deign to throw, for example, by vote-garnering speeches recommending innocuous prayers muttered aloud or silently in public schools. The pagans know how to use the tools of religion to their own advantage. A suggestion of piety, no matter how false or shallow, gains the votes of the ignorant. Nor is the peacemaker deluded into thinking that the warmongers will slink away once the Ten Commandments are hung in classrooms whether inscribed on plaques or in the *Congressional Record*. This patient realist recognizes the task of peacemaking for what it is: a steadfast, constant effort over against the violence in oneself and in society. Specious platitudes do not suffice. Peacemaking is a lifetime task of vigilance, a study of issues, an agonizing search for truth, and an abhorrence of fads or of the current costumes of emotional appeals. Steady, deliberate, in touch with a proper and healthy anger, thus does the peacemaker walk through whatever portion of history belongs to her/him.

There are many traits that characterize the peacemaker; this personality can be outlined by examining certain of the qualities that make up who the peacemaker has come to be. Peacemakers are in touch with the world in which they live. Naivete and ignorance do not earmark the woman or man who reads widely, listens to varying sides, thinks, and above all, chooses to be informed and involved. The anger that impels us forward is one that knows of and rankles at injustice; that is frustrated by the fact of tons of food stored or destroyed while families, even in this country, are hungry; that is offended by separate justice systems for the haves and the have-nots; and that realizes that private economic interests are the primary reasons why countries stand against the peoples who wish to determine their own political and economic futures. This is a disheartening litany. Some would call it the ill-formed raving of the liberal left. Whatever. Insularity was never announced as one of the marks of the church.

The peacemakers know the labels that will be sewn on their garments—naive, religious, unworldly, duped, good-hearted, sincere, unrealistic—yet they are haunted by the beatitude. The Catholic bishops of the United States have already received their barrage of such epithets after the publication of their intelligent, forthright, and fearless pastoral letter: "The Challenge of Peace: God's Promise and Our Response." Peacemakers welcome the courageous stand of their brothers. The summons to the beatitude has been sounded again. The serious issues are not dissipated by the name-calling, nor are the peacemakers daunted. The dismal possibility that efforts may come to naught is not a deterrent because here is a woman or man who sees life in a different context: All reality is located in the context of the reign of God. It has become impossible to experience history in any other way.

The peacemaker welcomes deep within a sense of dignity and personal confidence against which the taunts of scoffers are rendered ineffective. The self-demeaning person is easily overcome by the rhetoric of power. Clinging to their low self-esteem, they shuffle off to their corners of rejection immediately upon being challenged. We witnessed just the opposite in the peacemaker bishops who have stood their ground against powerful political figures. Self-hatred prevents people from being peacemakers. The greater the self-knowledge, the greater the lack of violence to oneself. Thus, the person who has undertaken the journey to the self is a likely candidate for becoming a peacemaker. In addition, self-knowledge allows us to come to the task with the least amount of vested interest or stupidity, because the fewer the ruses and personal ploys, the greater the potential for peacemaking unencumbered by a confusion of motives.

To the degree that self-knowledge is authentic and genuine, the peacemaker recognizes an inner tranquility resultant from the coincidence of opposites in exquisite balance. Simply put, within the peacemaker there is a personal balance of war and peace, of love and hatred, of dark and light, and of sin and grace. Here is a person of exquisite prudence and great courage; the integration of these opposites does not indicate a fainthearted human being.

The peacemaker has relationships outside the immediate family and community. When human beings congregate exclusively with their own, whether of color, creed, sexual identity, or culture, the tendency is to presume that "our way" is best or right or true. Only by meeting "outsiders" do we learn of the multiple ways in which humanity approaches the divine and the myriad of ways in which God reaches out to humankind. We learn people's motives and their backgrounds. Ghetto security is threatened, of course, yet the peacemakers perceive themselves infinitely richer. Their broadened perceptions of the earth's inhabitants enhance the probability of peacemaking. The self-journey is also augmented by multiple relationships. To meet others does not imply that the uniqueness of the self will be melded into every other, nor that we will become thistles blowing in the wind of every opinion and suggestion. The person who has undertaken the self-journey is magnified by relationships while the person who lives superficially loses personal significance in meeting another.

The peacemaker senses a growing urgency for the task of peacemaking, born, not of dread times, but of faith in the vision of the reign of God, as well as of a growing outrage at the smugness of the warlords. If these latter wore their armor externally, we might identify them instantly even across parking lots. But they look just like us and so often we are they. They wear business suits and jeans. The fine distinctions of the discernment of spirits become necessary to the peacemaker. What fruits grow on the trees of the militarists different from those on the trees of peacemakers?

Setting horticulture aside, we are brought to examine the paradigm which gives form to each one's choices. Dr. James Baines has delineated a paradigm of peace from a paradigm of power. Centuries ago, Paul, in addressing the Galatians, sought to alter the paradigm of power: "There does not exist among you Jew or Greek, slave or freeperson, male or female." Though Paul was able to overturn the power paradigm rhetorically and urge the community to a peace paradigm, it seems we and all the

earth's peoples still opt for a power paradigm. Having
not sufficiently overcome the first three polarities articu-
lated by the apostle, we have even created new ones:
Catholics or Protestants, Gay or Straight, Lay Women or
Nun Women, Doves or Hawks, People of Color or People
of No-Color, Feminists or Male Chauvinists. The list is
endless. One supposes that basic to the human condition
is our stunted sagacity that there must be "underdogs" if
we are to be "top-dogs." The peacemaker spies out a
power paradigm wherever it lies hidden within older or
more current language.

A paradigm is a mental referrent by, through, and in
which we structure reality. Once our paradigm, model, or
thought pattern is shaped every experience is brought to
it to be sorted and judged, otherwise our worldview would
be amorphous and in constant flux. It is healthy, however,
for individuals to bring their paradigms to conscious
scrutiny. Because the power paradigm has brought us to
the brink of world destruction, we are scrutinizing the
power paradigm at least in some of its manifestations.
Unfortunately, too many of us are blinded to the extension of this paradigm in our thought constructs. However,
by a gift of the Spirit we seem to be being led to a new
possibility for a peace paradigm. Perhaps Paul's words
can inch forward to acceptance in practice, beyond acceptance as a proper Christian rhetoric.

The peace paradigm refuses to juxtapose opposites and
thus to occasion further conflict and power struggles. It
defers continually to Paul's wisdom: "There is neither...
in Christ Jesus." Even the mention of the name of Jesus
as the One in whom all opposites are reconciled cannot
itself be used as a weapon of power against nonbelievers.

Multiple distinctions and differences in human society

are obvious and in themselves possess no intrinsic value; that is, it is neither good nor bad but indifferent to be woman or man, or to be one color or another. It is we who impute a particular value to being either/or and then force one of the polarities into an ascendancy for personal aggrandizement and advantage. Once established, our faulty value system solidifies our antipathies into invincible prejudice. Though others may inform us that prejudice is based on ignorance and fear, our paradigm is constructed. We have leveled society and now deal with the "powerless" according to our specifications. This positioning over against is the result of a power paradigm. It is the major way in which most of us experience and appraise reality. We co-opt every alternative into our granite-chiseled worldview.

The gift and immense beauty of Eucharist in Catholic Christianity is that all opposites stand together at the Table of the Lord acknowledging sinfulness, yet after offering one another a sign of peace eating the One Same Bread of equality and truth. What Eucharist signs is what the peacemaker works for each day. In the moment of Eucharist distinctions do not exist. The power paradigm is vanquished in sign. These statements more than hint at the breadth and magnitude of the Eucharist significance, at our obvious sin in ever restricting or limiting its reality, and at the demand placed upon us to extend Eucharist well beyond the hour of its celebration.

The peace paradigm has gradually become the thought construct of the peacemaker. It is what has impelled the peacemaker day after day. Because of their paradigm, peace is the way these persons look at the world. It is what they have become. This is why the true peacemaker is never dissuaded from the task by the exigencies of peculiar situations or is never captivated by the whims and fancies piped by the horns of plenty. The peace that Isaiah names as a vast river of prosperity typifies the limitless reservoir of self-knowledge out of which the peacemaker lives life.

Strategic planning for peace leads the adept peacemaker beyond merely muddling through tangled issues and intolerable circumstances. Peacemaking possesses particular skills and techniques. The peacemaker is trained through experience and listens carefully to the advice Paul offers the Corinthians: "We avoid giving anyone offense, so that our ministry may not be blamed." The peacemaker cannot chance harming the work of peace because of personal oddities. Thus is self-knowledge imperative.

The sparrows tell the peacemaker not to fear the forces of evil that can kill the body but never the spirit, while the vultures, as Jesus uses the simile, warn us to pay attention to the signs of the times. My mother had a wonderful expression for those who were never able to assess a situation and to get out of it while they were ahead. "They need a house to fall on them," she would say. The peacemaker does not wait for houses to fall before forming strategies and acting upon them after assessing the presence and the summons of Jesus in a given moment. The combination of trust and attention or perspicacity recommended by the birds seems to indicate the manner in which the peacemaker faces the world.

We watch with a growing pride and hope as different sorts of people from many countries assert themselves for world peace. They want a future for their children. They reject the prolonged explanations of Mutual

Assured Deterrence (MAD). They refuse to have farm-lands polluted by toxins, nuclear wastes, and buried missiles. They love their countries enough to speak out against excessive defense budgeting and the frenzied arms sales which have become the biggest sales item for and to national security states.

Perhaps, as so many young people take for granted, we are on the brink of the holocaust. Who can know? At least the peacemaker watching the sparrows and the vultures keeps vigil over against it. When others would despair, this person draws yet another creative possibility from the inner reservoir of peace. There is perhaps an effort toward negotiation yet possible.

The parables about seeds that Jesus told were meant to give confidence. Though we may not see the seeds sprout-ing and growing, wise farmers know the seeds will pro-duce thirty, sixty, and one hundred bushels. These stories were told by one who saw the ominous clouds gathering on his own horizon. He did not quaver before the impend-ing doom nor run for shelter and quit his mission. Jesus preached the power of God and the confidence we are to have that the promises given can be fulfilled. If we picture Jesus as merely going through certain redemptive gestures while possessing a beatific knowledge of the completed scenario, we cannot identify with his con-fidence. But if we know him as one threatened beyond imagining by the forces of evil, as one realistically fearful of the outcome of his life and as one overtaken by a sense of being abandoned by God, then his teachings about confidence give us some stability. We know only too well the magnitude of the disaster ahead. We are indeed fearful and yet we sing: "Patience, people. For the Lord is coming!" The peacemaker stands in the face of imminent catastrophe using every God-given power of mind and body to avert it. The peacemaker doesn't want the vultures to be a portent beyond the one presently suggested by Matthew.

CHAPTER NINE

Women and Men

God may well have overlooked bygone periods
when men did not know him; but now he calls on
all men everywhere to reform their lives.

God may well have overlooked bygone periods
when women did not know her; but now she calls
on all women everywhere to reform their lives.

God may well have overlooked bygone periods
when women and men did not know God truly;
but now God calls on all of us everywhere to
reform our lives.

Luke, in *Acts*, with variations

WE can hardly disembark without acknowledging the
presence of Noah and his wife (alas unnamed!) who were
indispensable to the work of creation that lay ahead of
them. We use our progenitors, passengers on this Ark, to
garner further insights that have bearing on the journey
to knowing the self. Their humanity brings us to the
question of androgyny and to the meaning of our work
of creation today.

Many of us seek to understand the God who is androgynous as well as the implications of androgyny in the
human person. The vocabulary by which we describe our
experiences of God betrays our theological quest, and the
changes we are making in our sexual role stereotyping
evidence our awareness that the androgynous person is
the most complete and perfect human person.

Androgynous combines in one word the Greek nouns

for man and woman; thus, even in construct the word conveys the duality and unity of feminine and masculine components. The concept of one who incorporates two is not a new idea; it antedates the birth of Jesus by several hundred years. We investigate the idea to derive from it whatever it offers in advancing the journey to the self; we examine the implications of an androgynous human being and by analogy, of an androgynous God.

The Chinese words *yin* and *yang* clarify our insights in discussing androgyny instead of our words feminine and masculine which carry such gender significance that we lose the point of the dialogue by language that invokes images of men and women persons. *Yin* refers to the qualities we ordinarily call *anima* or feminine. It does not indicate a female person. *Yang* names those qualities of *animus* or masculine; it does not connote a male person. The power that is in both *yin* and *yang* and in both feminine and masculine should be found in perfect balance in people who are female persons and in people who are male persons. The Chinese words, because they conjure no particular images in our minds, enable us to avoid the sexual role stereotypes immediately occasioned by the gender words: masculine = strong, active, sensate; feminine = sensitive, passive, intuitive. From these regrettable distinctions come the inanities we've lived with for so long: women are intuitive; men are not. Men take active roles in society; women, passive, and so forth. Unfortunately, even in C. G. Jung's descriptions of the thinker and the feeler, masculine language is used to depict the former, whereas Jung's nouns and pronouns immediately change to the feminine gender when he begins his description of the feeler. *Yin* and *yang* help us elude the trap of role stereotyping according to sex.

Throughout their histories, the believers of the great monotheistic religions have been for the most part limited to masculine nouns and pronouns, thus only to masculine or *yang* concepts by which to describe the One God. Today we, their descendants, are struggling to articulate a language for a God who is androgynous. It seems superfluous to insist: God is neither a woman nor a man; God is neither male nor female. Each of us knows this to be true. Nonetheless our speech betrays us. What we say is what we understand and know. Because we have always used only masculine language to name God, we feel awkward and embarrassed in addressing God as Mother, Lady, or Queen, the other aspect of the androgynous God whom we name Father, Lord, and King. Our heads tell us that God can be addressed with language other than that of patriarchy, but the accumulation of masculine words through centuries has driven from possibility a conceptualization of God as Queen. Yet there is in God that availability and relationship to us which is both maternal and paternal. There is that distance between God and us that allows us to say Lord and Lady, and there is that rulership in God over us that brings us to King and Queen. Yet our teeth are set on edge by the feminine terms. In addition, the feudal language poses a problem, not as much for the masculine terms, because we have grown used to them in a religious context, but the mention of the feminine consort brings only poor Guinevere to mind. Would that Lord and King spoke to us of Arthur! It would then be so much easier to disentangle these words connoting worldly potentates from our religious glossaries.

It might do us an immense amount of good if, for the space of one month, we read the psalms for prayer and

privately changed every masculine designation of the
deity to a feminine one. The activity thwarts us and so
upsets our religious stability that we can scarcely pray. I
urge us to it not so that we will think of God as female and
not male, but so that we ground within ourselves an
acknowledgement of God as androgynous and begin the
long slow journey to a language which suits our multiple
experiences of God's *yin/yang* interventions in our lives.

At a recent conference the people in our small groups
were asked to try to put in words a present experience of
God. To our mutual amazement, all of us described God
in *yin* terms, but this very haltingly. We did not possess
the adequate nouns and pronouns to name our experiences and so resorted to images, for example: 1) God is
the food and drink the prophet eats in order to go on the
journey; 2) God is like a cloud or like water. I swim in it;
3) God is a fellow sufferer, a gentle persuader; 4) God is a
vulnerable God, one immersed in our pain; 5) I find God
in nature, in the beatitudes; 6) God is liberator, one who
liberates me from within; and 7) God comes to birth
within me.

If we examine the language not for theological content
but for the experience of the man or woman, we find that
each had to struggle with examples from nature and
various human occurrences in order to find words for
their sense of *yin* in God. This fact is highly significant
and brings us to an overwhelming clarity: Our present
language for God is a meager, one-gendered vocabulary
which renders us impoverished and inarticulate when
we want to describe God who acts as *yin*. Our language
has limited us to the nouns and pronouns of *yang*. When
we need to name God as *yin*, we are forced to employ
numerous words, images, and examples because we have

no single nouns and pronouns to convey what we want to articulate of God's action. We feel awkward and incorrect using Mother, Nurturer, Lady, or Queen. Note that we can say with aplomb that God impregnates us with his strength; we are unable to say we suck at the breasts of her goodness. Oddly enough, in the last sentence it is not the word, breasts, that gives us pause; it is the pronoun, her. We could probably say with some ease that we suck at the breasts of God's goodness or of his goodness. Hopefully, the realization that we find it easier to put breasts on a masculine deity than to refer to God as "her," brings us to a conscious awareness of our lingual predicament.

The dullest among us senses the problem. What are the beginnings of solutions? First, we need to discover that power is resident in both the language of *yang* and the language of *yin*. Different, yes, but both powerful. The power of *yang* is the power of rain that pelts the earth and washes it clean. The power of *yin* is the power rain has to penetrate the earth and water it. *Yang* is the fire that consumes; *yin* is the fire that lights the way. *Yang* is the power of wrestling and struggle; *yin* is the power of surrender. In both polarities we discern great and forcible power. *Yang* does not typify power while *yin* will denote weakness. Because of our sexual role stereotypes we deny power to the feminine or *yin* and thus cause ourselves embarrassment when trying to depict the omnipotent God in *yin* terms. To discover the androgynous God and to name God in *yin* terms is not to deny power but to discover power of another sort. Both powers, *yin* and *yang* are creative. *Yang* produces; *yin* births. Both create to save, to give life and to nurture it. Both powers possess the potential of sin and destruction. *Yang* can flood the earth and destroy it; *yin* can so penetrate the earth with rain that the soil is inundated and unproductive.

We struggle for a proper vocabulary with which to typify that in the divine which is *yin*. We may have to use female designations for a while simply to get past our present limitations; we must work at the paucity of our language and move out of our confines. This demands, of course, admitting the paucity. One lady forged up to me after a lecture about the androgynous God to insist: "God is not a lady. God is a man and that's that. I was taught that God is a man and that is good enough for me. I hate all this new stuff since Vatican II."

The anecdote points to our linguistic malaise. Language describes reality. Let us not deceive ourselves that just because we use all masculine nouns and pronouns to name God that we, for a minute, worship a God who is androgynous, let alone a God who is in fact not male at all.

Now the point of all this is that we are at a time in our history when the need to emphasize the *yin* in God and the *yin* in the human person has become necessary. The Spirit is leading us to the change. God may well have overlooked bygone periods when we did not understand, but now God calls on all of us everywhere to reform our lives. Note that in these troubled times, we are calling upon the *yin* in God for comfort and preservation, for nurturance and assurance, for enlivening from within and for birthing new possibilities in us over against the rampant disorders we've brought upon ourselves. The peace paradigm discussed in the previous chapter is directly connected with the subtle but profound changes that have taken place in our experience of God. Because we know the *yin* in God, we can come in touch with the power of *yin* in ourselves and allow the peace paradigm to structure our self-understanding.

Multiple changes have taken place in our piety since the scriptures were opened to us after Pius XII's encyclical of 1943. We learned that our God was tenting with us and was not far off, over against, or a gigantic sky-god. Our experiences of the *yang* in God were altered as the Spirit revealed the profundity and extent of incarnation.

As a result the prayer and religious life of an entire people has changed. More than likely our Protestant sisters and brothers will testify to much the same phenomenon. When I asked a minister friend what they were doing after the Council of Trent while we were building and sealing off our mighty fortress, he replied that they had moved down the road just a short distance and were busy with their own fortresses. Without any mandate from us, God has led us through similar happenings to the new realizations and revelations of Providence.

We find ourselves praying with fewer *yang* images: "Fight against our enemies, O God," and with more *yin* images: "Walk with us, O God." We are comfortable with the androgynous God, but we lack a vocabulary to advert to this mystery in God and to name easily what God is doing in our midst.

Through the centuries, devotions came into prominence which allowed us to touch the *yin* aspect of God though we didn't call it such. Some examples are the devotion to Jesus as Sacred Heart, assuring us of Love, and the devotion to the Precious Blood, giving life for us with exquisite care. Our present devotion to the Holy Spirit in the Charismatic Movement is also a way in which we who have no language except that of *yang* have sought to typify our God with terms of power, not *yang* but *yin*. Perhaps it is only that *hypostasis* in God that we have called Father that evidences our limitations. We have not discovered androgyny in the creator, probably because the creation myths of the great monotheistic religions all depict a masculine sky-deity who creates from nothing, a mythology which permits its adherents a one-sided worldview.

It is unrealistic to presume that we who have been inured to centuries of masculine nouns and pronouns can switch to feminine ones without duress. It is unlikely and improbable that we shall or even ought to change in that manner. We seek the androgynous God, not a feminine deity, to replace a masculine one. Our current attempt at discovering the feminine or *yin* in the divine by attributing femininity to one of the *hypostases* in God, the Spirit, seems doomed for failure. It is as bad to speculate a Tom, Dick, and Carrie as it is to preach about Tom, Dick, and Harry. Both will lead to an inculpable tritheism. God is, was, and always will be androgynous by analogy. This means that in God can be located *yang* and *yin* and these in each *hypostasis* as well as in God pondered as One.

What we must do is what we are already beginning to do: refuse to use masculine nouns or pronouns to name God and choose inclusive language, such as Parent, or Mother and Father, or Creator. Search out the genderless terms of the scripture, Wisdom, Love, Truth, Life, Justice, Providence, and others, with which to call upon God. Avoid the use of pronouns or use the unfortunate his/her until androgyny becomes second nature to us. More importantly each of us must become consciously aware of the *yin* in God which we have always experienced, but for which we lack a proper vocabulary.

One of my most charming male friends will insist that in this discussion I have at last gone too far. To date, he has been able to walk with me theologically and to commend my insights and I, his. Shall we have to part company? I hope that the language of androgyny used analogously of divinity at least opens a possibility for intelligent dialogue.

The journey to the self eventuates in the discovery that the self is androgynous, that in each woman and man is *yang* and *yin* and that all humankind approaches God through both these aspects of our reality. Because of our acculturation as male or female, we may be more inclined to recognize one or the other power as predominant. Both in proper proportion, however, are essential to human maturation. In our journey to God we will know times of wrestling, struggle, and encounter as well as times of surrender and union of the nameless self with the nameless God. Both involve power. We so quickly connect weakness with surrender; more than likely there is greater power in surrender and union than in wrestling and differentiation. We know that part of us will always set others over against, while in each of us is the desire for union, oneness of being, and relationship. We must abandon the notion that one or the other of these behaviors is peculiar to men and the other to women. Both powers compose who each of us is. Both must be in perfect equilibrium for us to possess self-knowledge. We have that in us that pelts and washes clean; we have that in us that penetrates and softens. We have that in us that consumes and that which enlightens. The perfect man and the perfect woman has both *yang* and *yin* in good balance and in proper proportion.

The church community needs to emphasize *yin* in both its male and its female persons. The language of *yang* has resulted in the power paradigm. *Yin* holds within itself the power for the peace paradigm. We are at a critical juncture when our emphasis must be on that aspect of God that is *yin* and on that aspect in men and women that is *yin.* Perfection lies in androgyny, of course, but the time of *yin* is now. We must call upon all the powers within for peace, for surrender, for yielding, for causing to grow, for unity, for making one, for birth and for growth.

It is perhaps the female persons in the church who can point all this out to the community. A feminist theology does not mean female persons doing theology, though this work is to be sought and encouraged. It does not mean summoning goddesses from ancient mythology to worship these instead of Jehovah and Zeus, though a feminist theology might surely examine goddess worship to discover therein a search for *yin* in the nature of the divine. A feminist theology does mean, however, the discovery and articulation of androgyny in God. Because women have been acculturated to be comfortable with the immense power of *yin,* women and men should probe this acculturation to bring from it a wisdom to the community. The men and women of the believing community must listen to its women, discover their symbols, and analyse the ways in which women have approached the divine. This is a possible route to the revelation of the feminine, of *yin* in the divine. A language can be occasioned if men and women are concerned to construct it.

Without the intelligence, symbol system, and creativity of its women, the faith and wisdom of the church community is poorer by over 50 percent. We shall miss the articulation of *yin* that lies closest within the consciousness of women, not biologically, but because of the ambience in which we have lived our lives. This is changing societally and the change is a happy one. It is good that our children are becoming aware of their androgyny.

In some families little boys are permitted to rejoice in their powers of *yin* and little girls in their powers of *yang*. Perhaps the church is closer to the wisdom of androgyny and able at last to discern in God and to name with a proper language the eternal equilibrium of power in utter balance.

And perhaps we aren't. Patriarchy with its coordinate militarism promises sanctimonious vesture to its males. The power paradigm will die hard because there is so much to lose. Have we the self-denial and the trust in Providence to begin the journey to the androgynous self that is both church and individual? We shall be the poorer if we refuse the process. The Spirit who comes with peace comes with work to do. It is the work of creation.

A religious symbol which outlines our tasks for the years ahead is that of creation. When we can sum up our identity as church persons in a word or a phrase, then we feel we are not nameless or formless but have a purpose and a destiny. Our purpose and our destiny as a people are accurately designated by all the richness the creation symbol embodies.

This symbol comes to us from many creation myths. Our Judaeo-Christian religious tradition presents two such myths in the Book of Genesis: one from a writer who represents the formal, ritualistic priestly tradition, and one from a writer we call the Yahwist from the name which is given God. Both myths represent a masculine sky deity who creates from nothing. The creation myths of other religious faiths depict masculine and feminine deities involved in the creating thereby communicating an understanding of the Ultimate as androgynous at the beginning of time. According to some traditions and again an indication of androgyny, the earth is companion in the creating instead of being described as a formless wasteland and a dark abyss of nothing.

Myths are meant to communicate the truth that lies within the details of the various stories. Though we learn the myths as children, adults need to rediscover their messages. That our God created alone teaches that there were no other gods before this God. The creation myths of Judaism are primarily intended to depict the Oneness and Power of Yahweh over against the powerless gods of the other nations. We ought not read the Genesis myths for scientific data or even extensive theological insight into the nature of the deity. They tell us only what religious ideas the writer intended.

The myths of creation that now speak to some unconscious level within us are not the ones portraying the *yang* of God's singular omnipotence but those in which the *yin* of humanity and divinity together re-form the earth and birth a new order into the chaos that sin has caused. The ancient symbol calls us anew to embrace the earth and allow it to rejuvenate itself from our pollutants and disorders. We have been entrusted by God the creator with re-creating. The new creation is based on a paradigm of peace. We women and men undertake the creation now as a work of androgyny. The task is now. The symbol gives us an identity and a sacred charge.

If we read Genesis 1-11 carefully, we realize that the writers, given the void of their histories of sin, wanted to say that God had not intended things this way. God created and found creation good. It was we who sinned and turned the goodness of creation into hatred, genocide, pride, sodomy, and greed—all utterly other than what the benevolent deity had intended. The story of the Ark shows

God's gracious kindness in making covenant once again with sinful people. The writers of the creation myths antedated the history of sin and confusion to reveal mythologically God's different intent.

We recognize the tales of our sin as if they were the outlines of a movie we have seen many times over. We now know that the story of creation is not a one-time explosion of being millions of eons ago but a continuous act of salvation on into the present in which we are involved. The peace paradigm calls us to the task of creation/salvation. We have a sense that God summons us to give form to chaos and meaning to meaninglessness and so renew the face of the earth. Humanity and divinity have come together to cooperate in the new creation.

Certain creation myths tell of the sin, disorder, and evil that must be expurgated so that the new can arise. In a Hindu creation story, the god Siva dances on the back of the evil dwarf, and the rhythm of his hand drums and of his steps pulsate the form of the new. Beyond mythology we must be aware that the historical work of creating will cost us dearly. We cannot escape anguish, near despair, contentions of all sorts, ceaseless labor, and even death as we work to make a difference in our world. The historical work of creating includes the destruction of an old order before the new can arise, the purgation of evil so that good may evolve, and the dissipation of the power paradigm in each individual and in all societal relationships so that the designs of peace can take precedence. Ways of guaranteeing dignity and human rights to every woman, man, and child can only come about as oppressive governments are overthrown. A new economic order will be created only in the dissolution of the old.

In the religious history of humankind we learn that it is

usually only in crisis times that the new creation comes into being both in the individual, the religious community of the churches and in society at large. Over against internal and external chaos we are forced to exert meaning or yield to confusion and indecision. Over against the threat of nonbeing, we will claim being and purpose or risk destruction. Conflict challenges our identity; we will choose to deal with it deliberately or we will slough off responsibility and relax into a formless hedonism.

We can choose to create or we can dig our nuclear graves. We can meet conflct, change, threat, dissolution, the chaotic, and nothingness, and rise from our corporate lethargy to strain every shred of ingenuity in compelling the new from the decadent. Perhaps both capitalism and communism will be seen as having run their courses in our economic history, and we will be called upon to investigate the creative possibilities for an economic order that best serves all the earth's peoples. We are at such a juncture in history. The creation symbol assures us direction and purpose. It calls to the collective unconscious of conviction, destiny, and a genuine concern for our global sisters and brothers. Let no one think, however, that the creative tasks that lie ahead will be easy. Sin yields to the new creation only after a dreadful battle. We know this experience in our personal histories; in a global referent we cannot afford to be unaware of the birthpangs of the new.

In this context of creating we comprehend the imperative about knowing the self. Without self-knowledge we will wander for years in the narrow geographies of our small preoccupations. We live in fear and frustration with what might happen to us. We meet upsets and land on our heads and we never know why. Boredom swallows us up and we blame the tedium on everyone else. We worry endlessly about what others are thinking of us. We agonize about the future. We are excessively dependent on others for direction that should come from within. Mentors, possible loves, and friends are rejected; self-hatred, the correlative of lack of self-knowledge cannot admit them.

To know the self is to be able to let go of self-preoccupation and its debilitating loneliness. Self-knowledge tells us we are boring without this fact's destroying us. We have acknowledged the shadow side of ourselves. The new creation can be begun. The formless void of the unknown self gives way to significance and enlightenment. We know who we are, and we know our purpose for the few years in which we are responsible for this planet. Without self-knowledge, without symbols and myths to inform our steps, we feel purposeless and foolish. With an identity, a purpose, a commitment, and loved ones with whom to journey, we are rich indeed.

The cynics, the superficial, and the power brokers of the earth will smirk. The idea of a new creation within individuals and within society will be dismissed just as the peacemakers are dismissed by words calculated to demean: unrealistic, religious, sincere, out-of-touch-with-the-real-world.

Perhaps as one nears one's own human diminishment, the error of the myths of power and destruction are more clearly revealed. We are confronted only by the religious and, therefore, human choice. Where does human greatness lie? What and whom do we revere when our foolishness has evaporated like the morning mist? What happens when our own puny resources are exhausted? Where the power? Where the grace? Where salvation? Have we found it in evil and oppression? In greed and falsehood?

When these questions flood our consciousness, we remember that we have found truth in the two mites of the widow, in the woman who swept the whole house looking for what was important, in the neighbor who served and did not pass by, in the small efforts at creation rather than destruction, and in the act of gathering the animals and the humans into an Ark of friendship and love for safety and salvation.

The journey to the self will end with the possibility for self-denial, an unpopular claim in times of assertiveness training. But there is no real conflict. We can welcome self-denial and renunciation for the sake of the reign of God only if we are strong possessors of the self. If we know and love the self, we can offer the self-gift with freedom and graciousness. We recognize self-gift when we see it; the counterfeit gesture of self-denial has the ring of manipulations we've met before.

The message of Jesus, however, is not ultimately one of suffering and death. It is a message of life, a pearl to find, a talent to use, a seed to plant, a reign to extend, a love to give as bread, a neighbor with whom to walk, a city to enlighten, good news to be heralded, and an ark with which to make covenant. These metaphors speak of belief and action. Nothing sedentary and religiously comfortable here. The Ark was probably hot, odoriferous, and noisy, and Noah and his wife had a lot of cleanup work to do. The journey to the self resembles the progress of this trusty old vessel. Through floods and rain, noise and disorder, crowds and cacaphony, the journey continues. The work of the new creation is ours.

EPILOGUE

The Mountain Goat

But I—I Love to bound to the heart of all
Your marvels, Leap Your chasms,
and, my mouth stuffed with intoxicating grasses,
quiver with an adventurer's delight
on the summit of the world! Amen.
The Goat in Prayers from the Ark,
by Carmen de Gasztold

WHEN a lecturer asked us to name an animal with whom we identified, I chose a mountain goat. This sure-footed mountain climber has some instincts for journeying up steep and seemingly inaccessible paths. I liked its freedom and was glad to learn that hunters have a very hard time shooting it since it doesn't stay on any one precipice for very long but leaps securely onto the next.

We look back at the rocks that have been scaled on the self-journey. Frustration engulfs us climbers in having to admit that self-knowledge is not a peak able to be gained in a day or even in a year. There is nothing we can do to hasten the ascent except live each day with integrity and fidelity, testing every new plain for what it may disclose about the self. The journey lasts a lifetime, yet if we allow it, it is a journey which all along the way reveals the nature of God in the measure we attain to the self. The inner, nameless core of our being is the threshold of the divine. Just as we are, we have undertaken the journey and, through conflict, have reached further areas of self-knowledge; we have become more able to accept the unique creation that each of us is. To memorize and to recite our religious responses were simpler ways to deal with Holy Mystery than to continue steadfastly on the religious journey we have begun.

Finding an animal that is like us is a clever technique to talk to ourselves about ourselves. It is a simple test of self-knowledge. Which animal seems to go about life the way we do? We need not pick from among the ones gathered in these pages, but any from among those Noah assembled. How about a canary? Ask about canaries. Bring forward every fact you know about canaries. What does this ornithology tell you about yourself?

I met a man who was unable to do this simple exercise. He talked at length about German shepherds snarling, being tense and ready for battle, about being faithful and good caretakers. He could not bring himself to say: I am like that. Perhaps some will laugh at such a banal game. My guess is that this human German shepherd was never able to let anyone get too close to him. He sensed himself faithful to one master and to the ideals he espoused. He felt that people feared him, yet he wanted to be known as someone who could be counted on to care for whatever was entrusted to him. The German shepherd has unique gifts. The man was afraid to touch this level of self-aware-ness, let alone allow anyone else to catch a glimpse of his identity. Another fellow said right off that he was a giraffe. He was tall and gentle. He told us he felt he could see far off and help others get to places he could discern first. I've always felt sorry for the one who couldn't play. His imagination was trapped inside his defenses. He was afraid of self-disclosure, to us certainly, but probably most of all to himself. Think of the goodness brought to the community because of the German shepherds among us. We are deprived without them.

The exercise is significant because it is a nonthreatening way to look at some aspects of the self, laughing at the foibles and peculiarities, yet welcoming all the aspects of the complexity each of us is. If we ever become truly compassionate, it will happen on the day we delight in the cats, the lions, the dogs, the otters, the horses, the wrens, the mice, the ants, the sea anemones, the elephants, and the hippopotamuses. Each is a presence, a wisdom, a part of the creation the rest of us needs. But beetles aren't walruses and tigers aren't water loons. Sometimes we wish everyone was a mountain goat, but then we concede that zoos would be most uninteresting places!

From the vista of a high peak the mountain goat stops to look back on the way we've come. If we haven't built gigantic defense mechanisms against fear and hurt, conflicts great and small will have forced us to self-knowledge because they compel us to go beyond any plateaus where we have lingered. We can acknowledge the truth about our humanity; we are biodegradible earthlings, at once rational and irrational. We are sinners into whose powerlessness enters the Power beyond our limitations. We are lifted up on eagle's wings to meanings and confirmations we could never have gained alone.

The journey teaches us that our identity as followers of Jesus demands a total way of life, and we are forced to admit that Sunday is not the only day in which we have to deal with the implications of discipleship. In fact, church begins to feel less like an organization to which we belong and more like a group of people in and with whom we are to be allied on our journey. The passage or maturation from our ecclesiastical adolescence is a major conversion. A personal spiritual journey is underway. We can no longer presume from the pews that some religious elite is involved in Christianity while we must remain at our worldly tasks. The paradigm of what it means to be a church-member has been transformed by the Spirit of God. "Just tell us what to do and we'll do it," has changed to, "This is the way we think the community must go," a sentence which follows prayer and reflection, a genuine conversion of heart, and a growing sense of church as community of disciples. The memorized responses offered a vast theoretical explanation, but we know their content is to be interiorized. They have had to become part of who we are.

The mountain goat hopes that in ten years the sections about peacemaking or about the androgynous God will have become so much a part of our communal understanding that there will be a new context in which to read them. The mountain goat can leap to that hope, quivering, however, with the knowledge that the opposite could also have happened. We could once again have destroyed creation by our technology and by our insistence on the precedence of the power paradigm.

A recent television program showed the newer ways that managers of zoos care for the animals; the keepers befriend the animals, rewarding them for doing good rather than punishing them for misdeeds. Without pushing the idea beyond its usefulness, we learn that we may not misuse the earth or any of its inhabitants, nor may we abdicate our responsibilities as its stewards.

In the gathering darkness of our times, we need surefooted guides, women and men who will offer us a mature, spiritual vision over against chaos. The human spirit has within it all the possibilities for the new creation. After terrifying storms, the mountain goat leaps to a new horizon to behold there, blazoned across the sky, the sign of covenant. We have never been alone on the journey. Covenant was made long ago; it will never be revoked. The bow gleams through the clouds. The ark of the covenant, the dwelling place of God which humanity is, moves forward once again.

> "As long as the earth lasts, seedtime and harvest, cold and heat, summer and winter, and day and night shall not cease."